LJ's Cocoon

LJ's Cocoon

MY JOURNEY   *GOING TO PRISON*

THROUGH THE VALLEY   *SAVED MY LIFE*

TO THE WORLD OF OPPORTUNITIES

Lynard Joiner Sr.

To order additional copies of this book, contact:
Xlibris Corporation
1-888-795-4274
www.Xlibris.com
Orders@Xlibris.com
112055

Contents

DEDICATION

This book is dedicated to my mother, father, step-father, grandmother, children and my family.

I believe that we sometimes makes choices in our lives that take us places that we really don't want to go. But on the other hand, the journey can turns out to be a blessing in disguise. Being in prison to me is like being in another world. It's a mental thing not so much physical that you must deal with. Once you understand that, there no prison razor wire or bars that can confine you and keep you from soaring above your circumstance. Therefore with this mind-set, it's just was a minor set-back in order for me to move forward in life. This is just a bowl of LJ'S Life soup for you.

ABOUT THE BOOK

This book is nonfiction and contain country grammer and improper english. It is my life story as I recall it. Every episode and experiences told are true and have been written as I remember them. Most of the names, identities, and conditions have been changed to protect the moral character and/or privacy of the many individuals implicated. Conversation in this book have been written as I recall them, but they are not word-for-word but I've wrote them in a form that show and express the real feeling and meaning in the conversation without taking the truth away from what was said and the mood.

REASONS FOR WRITING THE BOOK

I decided to write my life story not for financial gain, fame, boast or to glorify being in prison; I will be the first to say there's nothing cool or hip about being in prison. I simply wrote this account of my life for self clarity to see where I have been, where I'm going and where I would like to go in life.

I also wrote my life story to let people know that despite the mistakes one makes in life, there is always another opportunity to make a positive influence in someone life as well as an opportunity to make a positive contribution to your community and society.

There's a true saying that say, "Your past is never done with you until, you are done with it." So don't let your past destroy your future.

CHAPTER 1

GROWING UP IN MISSISSIPPI

I was born in a small town called Louise, Mississippi. I have eleven brothers and six sisters. My family and I was very poor but rich in spirit, thanks to my mother. We lived in a three bedroom house that was made of wood and tin. There were only one bed in each room. As for us twelve boys, the one bed wasn't big enough for us all to sleep in it. It would only hold eight of us. There would be four of us at the head and four at the foot of the bed. I didn't like sleeping in the bed because my brothers stinking feet would be in my face. The other four that couldn't fit in the bed, made them a bed on the floor.

There was no water in the house, so we had to haul our water from down the road. We kept the water in two large fifty gallon barrels on our front porch. The water was used for drinking, cooking, washing, and bathing. Our restroom was outside behind the house. Some people called them outhouses.

It wasn't a good thing to have to take a number two in the middle of the night. First of all, it was about 30 yards behind the house and it would be piss black dark outside. It would be so dark that you couldn't see your own hand up to your face. You couldn't sit down on it. You had to squat over it.

In order for us to have enough food, we grew a large garden, raised chickens and hogs. Once a month, the government gave us butter, oatmeal, powdered milk, canned beef, peanut butter and cheese. I only liked the cheese because it made the best grill cheese sandwich in the world at that time.

My father who was a rolling stone, worked on the farm driving tractors in the field. He would get paid on Friday and we wouldn't see him until Monday and by that time, he would be broke as the Ten Commandments. Inspite of my father not taking care of his responsibilities at home, my mother always taught us to love and respect our father.

In 1969, my father was thrown off a tractor while working in the field which later caused him to be confined to a wheelchair. Even though my father were in a wheelchair, his lifestyle remained the same.

During the Christmas holiday seasoning of 1971, we lost our house to a fire. My father's friend Mr. Dont was working on our car and decided to come into the house to get warm. He had a small pan of gasoline in his hand with a car part in it. Mr. Dont sat the pan down in front of the fireplace and walked over by the table and grabbed a chair. As he got ready to sit down, he accidentally kicked the pan of gasoline over. Before he could grab anything to stop the gas from running into the fireplace, it was too late.

As soon as the gas hit the fireplace, the house quickly went up into flames because it was made of wood.

My mother immediately rushed us out of the house while my oldest brothers and Mr. Dont made sure that my father got out safe. After counting us, my mother realized that my brother Cheek was still in the burning house. By this time, the fire was at the front door and Cheek was in the backroom. My mother didn't even hesitate to go into the burning house to get Cheek.

On my mother's way out of the burning house with Cheek, she met my sister Libit at the door; trying to go back into the house to get her babydoll and shoes. My mother grabbed her and they came back to the side of the road where we was. Libit took off so fast that my brothers couldn't catch her.

We didn't save anything. Not even our dog Red, who was tied to the house. All we could do was stand, watch, and thank God that we were okay as our house burned to the ground. I recall hearing all of our fireworks going off, sounding like the bombing of Pearl Harbor.

Mr. Dont invited us to come and live with him until the Red Cross found us another house. Mr. Dont, his wife and his eleven children lived in a four bedroom house. Can you imagine thirty-three people living in a four bedroom house? The only thing that was good about staying at Mr. Dont's house was his bathroom was inside and there was water inside of the house as well.

Mr. Dont, his wife and my parents gave all of the household rules to us children. In so many words, they told us that we were one big happy family and don't fight each other.

We understood our double parent's rules that we were one big happy, but don't fight each other went in one ear and out of the other one. Everyday there would be a fight between us. Most of the fights was over their toys; in which we felt were our toys as well since we were one big happy family.

A few months later, we moved into our new house. Our new house was also made of wood and tin but the wood was covered with tar paper outside and wallpaper inside. There were only three bedrooms in our new house like in the old house.

Once again, the bathroom was outside behind the house. There was a pecan tree in the front yard and a peach tree in the backyard. These two trees were a blessing to us.

About seven months after we moved into the new house, it was destroyed by a tornado. I recall my mother going outside and yelling, "Ya'll come and look!"

She then ran back into the house and told us to get in the closet while they got down on the floor. A few minutes later, I heard the sound of broken glass and the house collapsed.

After the tornado had passed over, we came out of the closet to see what had happened. There were trees and power lines lying down everywhere. The neighborhood was in a mess.

Once again, we went to live with Mr. Dont and his family. They welcomed us back into their home with open arms. All of the house rules were the same as before.

This time our stay at Mr. Dont's house wasn't very long. In about thirty days we had a new house. Even though it was made of wood and tin, it was a nice house. It was bigger than any of our other houses. This time we had water in the house but there were no restrooms in the house. As always the restroom was outside behind the house. Our house was surrounded by cotton and bean fields.

There was a bridge over the top of a small lake of water about a football length away from the house. Since our house had been destroyed by a tornado, once before, we went down to the bridge and made us a tornado safe-house under it.

There's a saying that say, "When it rain, it pours." Shortly after moving into our new house, my mother decided that she had taken all that she could take from my father. She told us that she must go but she will come back and get us young ones.

As I got up the next morning, I asked, "Where is mom?" My brother Bob told me that she was gone to get us a new house.

My mother had left Bob with a telephone number so we could talk to her. My older sister Annie took on my mother responsibilities of cooking, washing, and teaching us our ABC's, colors, and how to count. She did a great job.

When I turned nine, my father began taking me to work in the cotton fields.

We would work from 6am to 6pm with the heat temperature reaching over 100 degrees and make only $5.00 for the whole day. But at the end of the day, we only got $3.00 because we had to repay the dollar back that we borrowed for lunch and gave the driver a dollar for taking us to the field. During this time, $3.00 went a long way.

In spite of the 100 degree heat temperature, it was fun going to the field.

There would be a fight or two every day in the field. Sometime the fights would be between two guys, sometime a girl and a boy or sometime two girls. I liked the fights between the girls, because if not both of their tops came off, at least one of their tops did and their little tits would be showing. Even though their tops would come off, they wouldn't stop fighting until someone broke the fight up.

After working all week long, we would go to the wrestling on Saturday. I loved to see the little midget, they was so funny. Now that I'm older, it's just was and is entertainment, it's not real.

Just as my mom said she would do, she came back for us. She only took the seven youngest children, which included me and left the others with my father to help him. I was happy that mom came back and got us young ones but I hated to leave the rest of the family behind.

As we arrived at our new house in Shaw, Mississippi; I was amazed at how close the houses was to one another. There wasn't a house within a half mile of my father's house. We stayed right beside our grandmom, Sadie.

At this time, my cousin Adie Jane who could pass to be white stayed with grandmom Sadie. She ran a little candy and snack shop out of the house. Even though the children in the neighborhood bought candy and cookies from her, they really didn't like her because of her light complexion. The kids in the neighborhood would call her white girl, honkey or cracker. After a week in the neighborhood, the kids stop picking on Adies Jane and became friends with us.

Our first day of school, we went to war with Adie Jane because a group of girls tried to jump her. It was my three sisters and Adies Jane against about a dozens of girls.

My brother Poorboy and me stood by to make sure that no boys got in the fight and made sure that those girls didn't get the best of them. There were days that boys would be fighting "Adie Jane and my brother and me would come to her rescue. It wasn't like she was scared of the boys, we just didn't want no boys fighting Adie Jane or our sisters.

After fighting almost every day for about two months, we finally earned our respect and they stopped picking on Adie Jane.

There was these two ugly sisters that liked me. Their names were Lorene and Corene. They would write me letters everyday asking me which one of them do I like. I would never answer their letters. One day during re-set they came over while I were talking with my friends and told me that I must pick one of them right now. I was so embarrassed. I said, "I don't like neither one of you ugly old girls. Now leave me alone!"

They then told me, "We don't like you either old nappy head boy," and walked off. All of my friends died laughing at me. I said, "That's not funny guys."

About two months before school ended, we went on a field trip. As we got to Memphis, Tennessee; Mrs. Smith told us that we are going to go to the Libertyland Zoo first and then to the fairground side. She also made it clear to us to stay with our group.

As we walked through the zoo gate, I immediately seen the lion and tigers.

There must been over two hundred different kinds of animals there. We had the opportunity to see them all. Out of all those beautiful animals, I was most fascinated with the peacocks, especially when they displayed their tail feathers as a fan. After seeing all the animals, we took a lunch break.

Once we finished lunch, we went over to the fairground side. The first thing that my friend and I ran to was the bumper cars. After getting on several of the rides, my friend Johnny Lee, Charles, Micheal and me decided to sneak back over the zoo side to play with the animals again. On our way back over to the zoo, we promised each other that we would stay together.

As we got over to the zoo, we went straight over to play with the peacocks.

We then went over to play with the monkeys and chimpanzees. Micheal then asked us to go see the bears. After being over at the zoo for about a half hour, we decided to walk back over to the fairground to catch back up with our group.

As we turned around to head back over to the fairground, we noticed that Johnny Lee wasn't with us. After walking and yelling for him for about five minutes, Micheal said, "let's split up and look for him."

I said, "No! Let's stay together so no one else will get lost." We walked for about twenty more minutes looking for Johnny Lee. We were too afraid to ask anyone have they seen Johnny Lee. So scared to death, we went back over to the fairgrounds. On our way back over to the fairground, we agreed not to say nothing about we went back over to the zoo, no matter what. I must admit, my heart was beating so fast.

Once we got back to the fairground and caught back up with our group, I felt just a fraction better but concerned about Johnny Lee. My friends and I kept looking around and hoping that Johnny Lee would show up before it were time for us to leave.

Finally, Mrs. Smith said, "Boys and girls, it's time to go home." At this time, my friends and I really became scared, because we didn't talk about what to say if Johnny wasn't with us when it was time to go. As we got on the bus, Mrs. Smith called roll to make sure that we all were on the bus. She finally called Johnny Lee name but he didn't answer. So Mrs. Smith asked each one of us, did we see him leave with anybody? We all said, "No mam."

About two hours later, the Memphis Police showed up with Johnny Lee. As I turned and looked out of the window, I seen Mrs. Smith and the police talking to Johnny Lee. My friends and me were hoping and praying that he didn't say anything about we went back over to the zoo. As he got on the bus, he gave us the thumb-up to let us know that he was okay.

The next day at school, the guys and me asked Johnny Lee what happened?

His response to us was, "I just wondered off" All we could do were say, "Man you had us scared to death." I will never forget this field trip as long as I live.

A month after school started back, we moved to Cleveland, Mississippi. I asked my mother could I stay with grandmom because I didn't want to leave my friends. She told me no because she had already signed me up for school.

As we turned into the neighborhood, all I could see were brick houses. We couldn't believe that we had a new brick home. As I got out of the car, there were a little midget standing outside next door. I stared at him for about a minute and then ran into our new house. It smelled just as new as it looked.

We had a large front and backyard which was great for us. All the children in the neighborhood began to walk by our house to check us out. I must admit that I wasn't as friendly to the children as the rest of my brothers and sisters was. Our house immediately became the hang out spot and later became the neighborhood park for the kids in the hood. We had a basketball goal, football and baseball equipment. My brothers and I also had a mini pool table and an electric football game in our room. My sisters had a easy bake oven and all kind of dolls. There would be mornings that when we woke up, our yard would be full of the neighborhood children. My mother didn't have a problem with that because all the kids in the neighborhood respected her and her rules while being in the yard.

At age of twelve, I won my first trophy in basketball in the eleven to thirteen year old league. The next year we lost the championship by one point. The following year I won the free throw championship for the fourteen year olds.

During the summer, I got a job working at the neighborhood's store. The store was owned by a preacher and his wife. They sold candy, cookies, chips, and small items that your parents might need before going uptown on the weekends. Believe it or not, they also sold beer, wine coolers, cigarettes and champagne.

I loved this job and the Browns loved and trusted me. In a week's time, I knew the business and started running the store by myself. I made a $100.00

a week. I would give my mother $80.00 every Saturday when I got paid. This job helped to shape and mold me into a responsible young man, and pointed me in the right direction toward my future career.

I am fifteen and I haven't got laid yet. There was a girl named Mary Ann who lived across the railroad tracks from me. She would come to the store every day to see me and then we would talk on the telephone for about a hour after I got off work. She invited me to come over to her house one night. She introduced me to her parents. Mary Ann parents' immediately took a liking to me because I was very respectful and I had a job. I would always say yes sir and no mam to them.

We used to stand outside on her front porch, kissing and grinding on each other. After kissing and grinding on each other for a week, Mary Ann told me that she wanted to have sex with me.

The next night after I got off work, I jumped on my bike and headed over to Mary Ann house.

I knocked on the door and she came to the door with her nightgown on. As I got inside, I asked her, "Where your parents at?" She said, "They are in the bed for the night." After we sat in the livingroom for about ten minutes, Mary Ann said, "Come on L. J., let's go into my bedroom." Mary Ann wasted no time once we got into her room. She pushed me back on her bed and got on top of me and began kissing me. I then started playing with her tits and grinding on her. A few minutes later she said, "L.J. come on. I'm ready for you." She then took her nightgown off. I noticed that she didn't have on any panties.

She then undressed me and we got busy. I really didn't know what I was doing but I could tell that it wasn't Mary Ann first time because she knew exactly what to do.

I didn't even use a condom. After we got done, I asked Mary Ann did she take birth control pills. She laughed and said, "Don't you think that it's kind of too late to be asking me now but I do?" Once I got dressed, Mary Ann told me to go look at the side of my neck in the mirror. As I looked in the mirror, there was a big red hickey on the side of my neck. After looking at the hickey on my neck, I went back into the bedroom and asked Mary Ann. "Why did you put this hickey on my neck?" She said, "I enjoyed your sex. It's good."

"Is that right?" I said with a smile on my face.

She then said, "Did you like it?"

"Hell yes I liked it. I will be over tomorrow for some more."

She just smiled and kissed me.

The next day at work all the girls noticed the big hickey on my neck.

They was saying stuff to me like, "Hmmm! Mr. Good guy, we know what you did last night." All I could do was smile and hunch my shoulder like what are ya'll talking about. The hickey that Mary Ann put on my neck sent a message to the rest of the girls that liked me; the message was clear if they wasn't trying to have sex, I wasn't trying to fool around with them.

Mary Ann and I had sex almost every day after we did it the first time.

Because I was the first one out of my posse to get laid, I used to call my guys lukewarm virgins; meaning that they were close to getting laid but haven't been laid yet.

One Monday night while watching the football game the phone rang. As I answered the phone, a young lady with a soft sweet voice said, "Hello, may I speak to L.J."

"Yea! This is L.J. speaking. Who is this?"

She said, "My name is Alberta. I am your girlfriend bestfriend."

"You must be Alberta. She told me that she gave you my number."

"She then told me, "I feel like I already know you because all Mary Ann do is talk about you all day long."

After talking with Alberta for about twenty minutes, she asked me, "Do ya'll have a stereo?"

"Alberta we may be poor, but we not that poor that we can't afford a stereo."

She then laughed and said, "I didn't mean it like that. Please excuse me."

She sounded so serious until I said, "I'm just joking with you."

"Ok. Would you please turn to 104 FM. They are getting ready to play this song that I dedicated to you and Mary Ann."

As I turned on the stereo, a nice slow love song was playing. Alberta then told me the name of the song and who was singing the song. The name of the song was, "If You Think You're Lonely Now," by Bobby Womack. Before hanging up the phone, Alberta gave me her address and asked me could I come meet her in person Friday or Saturday. I told her that I would come meet her Saturday night around 7pm.

As Saturday night rolled around a couple of my guys and I went over to Alberta's house. They lived down a long dark gravel road.

As I pulled up in Alberta driveway, their porch light came on. I blew my car horn a couple of times and someone stuck their head out of the door and said, "Who is it?"

"My name is L.J. Alberta there?" A few minutes later, a slim but fine red bone came out on the car porch. We got out of the car and walked up to her.

She immediately said, "Hello. You must be L.J."

I said, "How did you know which one of us was L.J.?"

She said, "Mary Ann described you to a T to me."

I guess she did because I am L.J. This is my friend O.D. and this is my friend Shane."

"It's nice to meet you guys. Would ya'll like to come inside?"

I said, "Sure."

As we got in the house, Alberta little sister said, "I'm going to tell dad that you had these boys in this house." Alberta then hit her in the back and told her to go in the bedroom and tell that. About five minutes later, a young lady with big pretty brown eyes came into the livingroom. She had on her school gym shorts and T-shirt. My guy Shane said outloud, "Damn! Who is that?"

My guy OD and me just looked at him. After realizing what he had said and done, he said, Excuse me."

We all just laughed at him. Alberta then introduced her to us. "This is my sister Gladys Ann." She was built like a young Tina Turner.

After being at Alberta's house for about a half hour, her parents drove up.

Her mother came in the house first and said, "How are you young men doing?"

We all said, "We are doing ok mam." As Alberta's father walked into the house, he stopped and looked at us.

"Who damn car is that in my driveway?" He said, "Go move it right now and don't ever park in my damn driveway again?"

I said, "It's my car sir. I will go move it right now sir." Once I got back into the house, Alberta apologized to me for the way that her father talked to me. I told her that it was cool but it really wasn't but my mother always told me to respect my elders.

Alberta, Gladys, me and my guys got up and went outside. Alberta was a sophomore and Gladys Ann was a freshman. We talked for about a hour before we asked them would they like to go to the club with us.

The both of them said it at the same time, "Crazy Joe will kill us if he just heard we was at the club."

"Who is Crazy Joe? I asked them.

"L.J., that was Crazy Joe that went off on you." Gladys Ann said.

O.D. and Shane both busted out laughing at me. "So ya'll think that was funny, huh?" We then told Alberta and Gladys Ann that we would be back next Saturday.

That Monday night, Mary Ann called me and told me that Alberta gave me and her a compliment . . . she told me that Alberta said that me and her was a perfect combination. I told Mary Ann that I felt the same way about us.

Mary Ann then told me, "I just can't get enough of you. I need you to come over tomorrow when you get off work." I will be there as soon as I get off. I then gave Mary Ann a good nigh kiss through the phone.

The next day after I got off work, I jumped on my bike and went over to Mary Ann crib. As I rode up to the house, Mary Ann was standing out on the porch. I walked up on the porch and gave her a hug and a kiss. We then went into the house and into her bedroom. We talked about Alberta and my encounter with Crazy Joe. As I was telling Mary Ann about Crazy Joe, she stopped me and said, "Baby, I forgot to tell you about him. He don't really like no young men at his house, especially when he is not there." The bad thing about it, I had two of my friends with me. They laughed at me just like she was doing. After Mary Ann got done laughing, we got busy.

After being over Mary Ann house for nearly two hours, I told her that I must head home if I were planning to get up for work because I was tired. I then gave her a kiss and got on my bike and headed home.

The next day I woke up around 1:30pm and I had to be at work around 2pm.

As I walked into work with sleep in my eye, Mattie and Rosie said, "We wasn't expecting you to get here on time."

"I had a rough night last night doing the inventory that you guys forgot to do."

"We didn't forget. Mr. Brown told us that he wanted you to do it," Mattie said.

"Is that right?"

"LJ. We are not joking, he said it."

"Ok. I'm done with it. Ya'll can go. I got it."

That day at work, I couldn't hardly keep my eyes open. After being at work for a hour, my supervisor Mrs. Brown walked into the store. She then asked me, "Have the Wonder Breadman showed up yet?"

"No mam. He haven't came yet."

Mrs. Brown then asked me; "L.J., are your mother making any of those good beans and cornbread today?"

"I don't know Mrs. Brown but I can go check and see for you." This was my opportunity to go take me a short nap. My eyes was red as a coal of fire.

So Mrs. Brown asked me, "What are taking for that cold you got?"

I said, "Nothing Mrs. Brown. I will be okay after I get a little rest."

"L. J., you can go get you a couple of hours or whatever you need of rest if you want to. Just make sure that you bring me some beans and cornbread back if your mother made any," said Mrs. Brown.

I went to the crib and got me about three hours of sleep. I then made Mrs. Brown a bowl of beans and cornbread. As I got back to the store, Mrs. Brown couldn't wait to leave with her beans and cornbread. I was now back to life and ready to work.

As Saturday came around, I went to see Alberta and Gladys Ann again. On my way out to their house, I stopped by Shane's crib and grabbed him. I also stopped by O.D.' s house but he wasn't home. I then made my way to Alberta's house.

Once we got to the house, I made sure that I didn't park in Crazy Joe driveway. Shane and I got out of the car and knocked on the door. Gladys Ann came to the door and invited us in. As we got in the house, Alberta was in the kitchen frying chicken and making mac & cheese. I must admit that her food smelled and looked good.

I was hungry but my pride wouldn't let me say yes when they offered me the food. I did ask her for a glass of water but she brought me a glass of red Kool-Aid.

Guess who came home about ten minutes later? Yeap! Crazy Joe came home and caught Shane and me at his house again. He walked in the house and said, "I see you boys are here again. You guys must call and check to see if I am here before ya'll come over." Neither Shane or me said anything.

A few minutes later, Alberta's mother who was in her bedroom all of the time, called out and said, "Joe, would you leave these boys alone. These are the girls' friends and they are some nice respectful young guys."

Crazy Joe then said, "I bet they are. I been their age before."

Mrs. T's then asked me, "Baby who is your people?"

"My mother name is Mary Sanders and my grandmother is Mrs Sadie Rush."

Mrs. T's then said, "Your mother is not the Mary Sanders that lived in Renova?"

I said, "Yes mam. That's my mother." Mrs. T's then called Crazy Joe and said, "Joe, guess who son this is? This is Mary Sanders son, who used to live in Boatwright. She got a brother name Will, Junebug, Gene and Richard. I forget the other boy name."

Crazy Joe then told me, "Boy, me and your Uncle Junebug used to hang out together when we was young men. We went to McEvan School together."

Once Mr. Joe knew who my people were, he had a whole new attitude toward me and my guys. "My Uncle Junebug must've used to kick his tail when they were younger," I said to myself.

About two weeks later, I was at Alberta house and her brother, who I haven't never met walked into the house. As he seen the "c" on our jackets, he immediately stopped and said, "You guys need to get up out of here and go back on the white side of the town."

Alberta then said, "These are my friends and they don't have to go nowhere."

"Alberta, we are going to leave because we don't want to disrespect ya'll house," I said.

She then grabbed me by the arm and said, "This is not his house. Dad and mom knows that ya'll be coming over here."

He then said, "You chumps better not be here when I get back."

"Alberta then said, "Kenny, they will be here when you get back."

"Alberta, I don't want to fight your brother, especially in ya'll house. So I am going to leave."

Shortly after Kenny left, Gladys Ann came home from work with her Wendy's outfit on. Alberta immediately told her what was going on. Gladys Ann told me and my guys that we didn't have to worry about anything.

So we sat back down and went back to watching tv. About fifteen minutes later, Kenny came back in the house and said, "You chumps come outside and we can do whatever."

My guys and me got up and walked outside. As we got outside, there was about seven guys standing out there with baseball bats and sticks.

I then walked up to Kenny and said, "We not looking for any trouble but we can handle this like men." The rest of the guys that was with Kenny ran up on us. I then said, "Put down the bats and sticks and we can get it on. It's eight of yall and four of us." The next thing I knew, my guy Shane had stole on one of the guys. I then rushed Kenny and threw him on my mother's car. While I had Kenny hemmed up on the car, one of the guys hit me in the jaw. He got a good punch in on me. I let Kenny go and grabbed the guy that hit me in my jaw. I picked that little joker up and body slammed him so hard.

About ten minutes into the fight, Alberta parents' drove up. All of Kenny's friends took off running. Kenny walked into the house to change his clothes. We all was wet and muddy because it had rained early that day. Mr. Joe and Mrs. T's didn't notice the mud and blood that was on me. My guy and me stayed outside. Once again Alberta apologized to me and my guy. and promised us that we wouldn't have any more problems with Kenny and his guys.

While we were standing outside, Kenny came back outside to go catch up with his boys. About five minutes later, Kenny left. We told Alberta that we was going to change our clothes.

As I pulled off from Alberta house, I turned my headlights on bright. A few minutes later, we seen Kenny and his guys standing in front of the store that was up the street from his house. I immediately whipped into the store parking lot and we jumped out on them and they ran up in the store. The young lady who was working in the store told us that if we came in the store, she was going to call the police.

A couple of days later, I called Alberta to see what was happening with her. She told me to feel free to come see her and Gladys Ann.

Kenny had Alberta to call me and tell me to come out to the house so we could talk. As I got to Alberta house, Kenny was standing on the porch. I got out of the car and said, "What's up Kenny? You want to talk to me?"

He said, "I just wanted to apologize to you and your guy for that night we got into it."

Kenny, I really didn't want to fight you because your sisters are my friends and your parents know my family. But I still want to fight that guy that hit me in my jaw that night."

Kenny then told me that I broke dude arm when I body slammed him that night. In order to make a long story short, Kenny, me, and my guys became cool.

Now, that the summer was coming to an end, Kenny tried to talk me into switching from Cleveland High to East Side High School but I told him that I couldn't do it. Even though both schools were black and gold, I was happy with being a Wildcat instead of a Trojan.

Once school started, Mary Ann and my relationship began to change because we went to different schools. I played football and I worked to 11 pm. I did my homework in study hall, which was my sixth period class.

One day during lunch break, my guys and I was standing in the school parking lot talking when a group of white boys approached us. The biggest one in the group said, "Which one of you niggers name Ledale?" Neither one of us responded. Once again, he said, "Which one of you niggers is name Ledale?"

Finally Ledale said, "I'm Ledale."

The big whiteboy then said to Ledale, "Nigger! You grabbed my girl butt."

Ledale then said, "No. Our lockers are side by side and we bumped into each other. I told her I was sorry."

"Nigger, I know you are not calling my girl a lie," he said.

Ledale kept trying to explain to him what happened, so I said, "Ledale, you have told him that ya'll bumped into each other and you told her excuse you.

Let's go, the bell is about to ring." As we began to walk off, the big whiteboy jumped on my back and began choking me. I tried to throw him over my back but I couldn't, so I bit him and he let me go. He then rushed me but I side stepped and tripped him. I quickly jumped on top of him and started beating him like a madman. There was no way that I was going to let him get up.

Shortly after I started beating him, everybody started yelling break it up, the teachers are coming. By the time they separated us, the teachers as well as the school principal was standing there. The principal told the both of us to go to his office.

As Mr. Buckley came into his office, he said, "Do you young men want to tell me what that fight was about?" Neither one of us said a word. We just kept gritting at each other. So Mr. Buckley gave us a choice. He told us that we could either take three licks or get a two day suspension. We both took the two day suspension.

I never told my mother that I had got suspended. I got up for school just as I did before I got suspended. I would ride the bus to the school and then walk over across the street to the arcade and play games all day. Once I got hungry, I would walk over to a Pic-A-Bit shop and grab some chicken, jojo potatoes and a jungle juice. The school let out at 3pm, so the bus would always show up about five minutes early. I would walk back across the street to the school and get on the bus.

That Friday night, coach didn't let me dress for the football game because of the suspension and missing two days of practice. We lost the game 38 to 10.

My mother lost her job and we went to stay with our father, who had moved to Springfield, Illinois. I didn't tell Mary Ann, none of my friends, nor my football coach I was leaving.

CHAPTER 2

MOVING TO ILLINOIS

As we made our way to Springfield, Illinois, my brother Bob made sure that we all was woke so we could see the lake. About fifteen minutes later we pulled up to my father house.

There were niggas standing on the corner selling dope, shooting dice, and prostitutes running from car to car. The neighborhood was also full with children. I remember seeing two fat twin brothers with afros standing out in front of two black 77' Lincoln Continentals.

They were Ronald and Donald, two fat pimps. They had the pimping business on lockdown on Edward and Jackson Street. Most of their prostitutes was between the ages of fourteen to eighteen. It was like I was watching television. I hadn't never seen anything like this before in real life.

After a few days or so I began moving around in the neighborhood. While walking around the corner from the house, I ran into a couple of girls. They introduced themselves to me. One of their names was Nancy and the other one name was Cookie. I then told them that my name is L.J. and I am from Mississippi.

They said, "We can tell that you are not from here. You sound like you are from down South somewhere. I just smiled and said, "That's where I'm from. Deep down South."

They both then said, "M. I. crooked letters, I. crooked letters I. PP. I."

Nancy then said, "Cookie, this country boy is kind of handsome."

I smiled and said, "Thank you. You two are cute." I must be honest with you, I lied to them. Nancy looked like Buckwheat twin sister and Cookie looked like she could be J.J. identical twin. I just didn't want to hurt their feelings.

After talking with them for a few more minutes, I said, "I will see ya'll later." I then slowly made my way back to the house.

The next day a few of the kids in the neighborhood came over to the house and introduced themselves to us. One of the guys name was Cub and we became good friends.

The next day Cub and I walked all around the neighborhood. He showed me the donut shop that was around the corner from the house on Eleventh Street. We also stopped by the pool hall on Twelfth and Jackson. As we were coming out of the pool hall, a young prostitute asked us to buy her a sandwich and she would take care of us later around the corner in the alley. My guy Cub was about to do it but Ronald and Donald came around the corner and that prostitute took off running like she had seen a ghost.

Cub said, "Damn man! I was about to get you your first real blowjob."

I said, "Stop playing man. She want $20.00 not $2.00."

Cub then asked me, "How do you know how much she charge?"

I said, "I'm slow but not that slow."

After leaving the pool hall, we walked back to my father house.

The next day after Cub got out of school, he came over to kick it with me.

He told me about all of the beautiful girls at his school. He asked me to come to his school but I told him that we were going to move in a couple of months.

After I told him that I had a nice B game, he told me that they had the best basketball team in the city. I said, "Is that right?"

"Just come and see. We got a center name Melvin Lee, he's tough."

"I will ask my sister and I will let you know."

Cub then told me that I could use their address if I need to.

After talking about basketball for about a hour, we walked up to a club called the Metro. As I was walking into the Metro, my brother who went by the name, the Mississippi Kid, was coming out. He asked me where I okay and I said, "Yeap."

Once we got inside of the Metro, it smelled like a weed factory. I went to coughing and my head went to hurting. I told Cub, "I got to go outside man. I can't stand this stuff."

He went to laughing at me and said, "Let's go country square."

I said, "Watch your mouth man."

Cub then said, "I'm sorry man, but I was just joking with you."

On our way back to my father house, Cub said, "L.J., I'm not sorry for calling you a country square. Prove to me that you not a square."

We then stopped by some female house. As we knocked on the door, a pretty young lady came to the door and said, "Look who the wind blew by." She then told us to come in. She then called her sister and told her to come and look.

Her sister then came into the livingroom with some red hot short pants and a white top on. Her nipples was hard and pointed. She was fine and sexy' as she could be. She was a brickhouse for real.

Cub then introduced me to them. One of their names was Christine and the other one name was Geraldine. They both said, "Hi L.J.," with a sexy smile on their face.

I said, Hey, how ya'll doing?"

Cub and Christine walked into the kitchen. Geraldine then said, "L.J., excuse me but I need to go change my top."

I then said, "You are fine with the one that you have on."

She then said, "Thanks, but I don't think what I have on is appropriate to have on around a stranger. Please don't take this the wrong way. I wouldn't never came out here dressed like this if I have known ya'll was out here."

I said, "I understand where you coming from." But I noticed that she didn't go change her top. She then asked me where I was from. I told her that I was from Cleveland, Mississippi. "So where are your parents," I asked? She told me that her parents was gone to St. Louis for a few days. I then said my favorite response, "Is that right?"

A few minutes later Cub came out of the kitchen and told me chill for about a hour. I said, "I'm cool."

Geraldine then said, "Don't worry. He's in good hands."

Geraldine then got up and turned on some soft slow music. As she came back to the loveseat, she told me, "I broke up with my boyfriend yesterday at school."

I said, "I'm sorry to hear that. I hope ya'll makeup."

"I don't want him no more. He has cheated on me too many times, she said.

She then asked me, "Do you have a girlfriend?"

I quickly said, "Nope! I only been here for about a week."

She then grabbed my hand and said, "Would you give me a hug?" I gave her a hug but for whatever reason, I was nervous. Nevertheless, before I knew it, we was kissing. We both stopped, looked at each other, and wiped our mouth.

She then said, "I am sorry. I don't normally kiss guys on the first day, especially a stranger."

I then put my hand on her leg and kissed her.

A few minutes later, we went into her bedroom and laid on her bed. Once again, we began to kiss and I ran my hand under her top and started playing with her tits. The next thing I knew, we was about to get busy and she asked me, "Do you have a rubber, a condom?"

I said, "No, I do not. She then said, "It's bad enough that I am kissing you and I don't even know you. I can't have sex with you, especially without a condom."

I was mad as hell with her but I played it off by saying, "It's cool, I understand." She then put her top back on and got up.

Just as she put her top on, her sister walked into the room. She said, "Excuse me, I didn't know ya'll was in here. I thought ya'll was outside."

As we came out of the room, Cub said, "L. J. you are not a square by a long shot."

Geraldine quickly said, "L.J., tell him that we didn't do anything but talk."

"She's right. We didn't do anything but talk man," I said.

Geraldine then called me into the kitchen and asked me not to tell Cub anything about what we did and what we almost did. I made her a promise that I wouldn't say anything to Cub about what we did or what we almost did. She then gave me her seven digits and told me to call her when I get home. She then kissed me and smiled at me.

Cub then said, "L.J. Lets go man. You can come back to tomorrow."

"Here I come man," I said.

On our way back to the house, Cub tried to make me tell him what Geraldine and I did but I kept my promise that I made to Geraldine. But on the other hand, Cub told me exactly what happened. If I didn't know any better, I would have thought he was peeping in on us. I denied everything except she gave me her telephone number.

As soon as I got home, I walked down to the payphone and called Geraldine. I talked to her for about a half hour. I told her that Cub tried to get me to tell him what we did, but I didn't. As I got ready to get off the phone, Geraldine asked me, "So what's going to happen with us now?"

I said, "I don't have no girlfriend. So you let me know whether you are going back to your boyfriend or not."

She then said, "I told you that I don't want him anymore."

"Check this out, I will be over tomorrow around 5:00 pm, bye."

The next day, I showed up at Geraldine's crib at 5: 00 pm. She must was looking out of the window because as I got ready to knock on the door, she opened the door and invited me in. She gave me a kiss and told me to have a seat. She then asked me, "Where is Cub?"

"I don't know," I said. A few minutes later, her sister Christine came into the livinroom and asked me the same question.

"Where is Cub?"

I nicely said, "I really don't know."

Christine then went back into her bedroom, and slammed her door.

"Geraldine then said, "So what's up with us?"

"Listen Geraldine. You are a nice looking girl and I think you will be a good girlfriend for me but I am not looking for no trouble," I said.

She then said, "So I guess you just want to get you some city pussy and that's it?"

"So you are trying to judge this book by the cover hun? I'm not like your exboyfriend or nobody else. If I wasn't trying to get to know you, I wouldn't be over here now, I said.

Geraldine then said, "I'm sorry. You are right. I don't really know you, so I shouldn't had said that about you."

She then began kissing and touching me below the belt. We then got up and went into her bedroom.

As we got into the bedroom, Geraldine asked me, "Do you have a condom? If not, you need to go get one now, she said.

I immediately reached into my pocket and showed her the condom that Cub gave me on our way home last night.

Geraldine and I then wasted no time getting busy. Once we got done, we decided that we was going to be boyfriend and girlfriend, but take it day by day.

Two days later, Cub and I went over to Geraldine and her sister house and they told us that they was moving to St. Louis, Missouri tomorrow. I then gave Geraldine my father address and promised her that I would stay in contact with her.

I never heard from Geraldine again, maybe because my father moved to Brandon Drive a week later.

As we pulled up into the project, there was people hanging out everywhere.

They were staring at us like they haven't never seen black people with a u-haul truck before.

Once we got all the furniture and stuff off the u-haul, we came outside and stood on the porch. There were three girls to every boy in this project. While standing out on the porch, several young guys walked up and asked us did we need any help. We told them thanks but we okay. They then introduced themselves to us. There name were Pete, Earl, Donald and Maine. Pete and Maine were boxers and they both were Golden Glove champions.

It didn't take long after moving into Brandon Drive for my father house to become the hangout spot.

There was a double side basketball court in the back of the project. After being in the project for a few days, I decided to go play some ball. As I walked around to the basketball court with all eyes on me, I yelled, "I got next if nobody call it."

Just as the game ended on the right side, my brother Poorboy walked up. So we grabbed three of the guys off the losing team and said, Let's go."

My brother Poorboy scored the first three baskets for us. They then went up 7-5. I then scored our next four baskets. We ended up beating them 16-11. We won the next three games before losing.

The next day while playing basketball, a red Dolman Pincher dog ran wild onto the court. We all took off running and the dog attacked a five year old boy before the twelve year old owner caught him. The owner of the dog was Pete 'the boxer' Lil brother. Once he grabbed the dog, Pete walked up to him and hit him with a quick two piece and told him to take the dog into the house. He then told Pete, "that didn't hurt me."

"Pete just looked at him and laughed.

That Friday night, there was a party at the Brandon Green Building Community Center. Poorboy, my cousin Henry and I decided to go check the party out. The party was packed with girls.

Even though I had two left feet when it came to dancing, I got several dances mainly because I was a new kid in the neighborhood. I also came up on seven female numbers. Everyone of them lived in the Brandon projects, except two of them. They lived around the corner from the project on 25th Street.

Right before the party ended, I slow danced with this girl named Loreta.

The perfume that she had on was so strong that it almost took my breath. On top of that, she had the nerve to pull me closer to her and grind on me; talking about I just love this song, "Tonight is Tonight." I couldn't wait until that song ended.

I didn't say anything to her, I just went outside to get some air. There was four girls standing about five feet from me laughing. They told me that she always smell like that.

I said, "Is that right? I sure hate it."

Those girls fell out laughing. I don't know whether they was laughing at what I said or the way that I said it. Whichever one it was, it was real damn funny to them, but not me.

Poorboy and Henry walked by me with two females they had come up on and said, "We will catch up with you later."

A few seconds later, a true bad redbone walked up to me and said, "Hi L.J., my name is Annetta and I am your next door neighbor." I was so amazed at how sexy and beautiful Annetta was that I forgot to ask her how did she know my name. She was built like a Coke bottle. Annetta and I then walked to the house together. We stood outside and talked for about forty-five minutes before her boyfriend pulled up.

As Annetta's boyfriend walked up to the house, she introduced me to him. I shook his hand and then told Annetta that I would holler at her tomorrow. She then said, "It was nice meeting you L.J, I will see you tomorrow."

The next day Annetta came over to the house and asked me to take a walk with her. We walked around for a while and then we stopped by Dairy Queen.

Instead of me buying Annetta something, she bought me a banana split with carmel, whipped cream, chopped nuts, and a cherry on top of it. She then told me, "This is my favorite and I like it just like this; if you know what I mean.

Opps! Please excuse me, that slipped out."

I just looked at her, smiled, and said, "I know what you mean." Only if she knew what was running through my mind on that time.

As Annetta and I was on our way back from walking, we ran into my friend Cub. "What's happening L.J.?" Cub said.

I said, "I'm cool man. This is my next door neighbor Annetta."

Cub then said, "I know Annetta with her cute stuck-up self."

I'm not stuck-up," said Annetta.

"So what are you doing later?" I asked.

Cub said, "Nothing."

I then told him to swing by and I live at 29 Brandon Drive. We then hugged and went about our business.

Once we got back to the project, rumors was already in the air about us. As much as I wished they were true, they wasn't. Annetta and i were only friends, even though we hit on each other. Our friendship was more important to us than our flesh desires.

With about four and a half months left in school to go before school ended for the summer, I started going to Southeast High School. My brother Poorboy and I walked to Southeast School that Monday. As soon as we walked through the school door, all eyes was on us. We stuck out like sore thumbs.

Once inside the school, we went into the cafeteria and grabbed us some chocolate milk, cookies, and some fruit. While sitting at the table eating, four nice looking girls walked over to the table and asked us could they join us. We said, "Sure have a seat." They then introduced themselves to us. One of their names was Chris, Diann, Glory, and Brenda. We then introduced ourselves to them.

Believe it or not, they somewhat knew us because their grandmother house is right beside my mother house where I grew up at. During the summer, they used to come and visit their grandmother and we would conversate with them. They then showed us around the school. Every morning we ate breakfast together. They treated us like we was family. I also knew their brother Tommy, who played basketball for the school.

After being at Southeast for a few months, I dropped out of school. At this time Mr Dont and his family had moved to Springfield. Since Mr Dont sons and I had grew up together we knew each other very well. We would steal and fight together. It was nice to be re-united with Mr Dont and his family. We lived in separate houses but we would become one big happy family again.

It's now 1981 and we now live in a project called the John Hay Homes.

This project was packed with kids and infected with street gangs, drugs, prostitutes and stick-up boys. It was like a small branch neighborhood of L.A.

My second day in the project, I saw a man kill a man over a cigarette. I was like, "Wow!" I didn't hear anyone say call 911 or the ambulance. As a matter of fact, during this time the police would just ride through the project every blue moon. There was Housing Authority security guards who carried sticks but the residents and outsiders carried guns and knives. Those security guards was scared to death and I couldn't blame them.

About fifty yards across a railroad track was a small project called, the Jeffersons' project. It was very small but full with teenage girls. All of the Jefferson project kids hungout in the Hay Homes, even though it was dangerous because it was the spot.

After being in the project for about a month, I had about eight females trying to get with me. There was Missy, Elouise, Joyce, Nise, Penny, Chris, Patricia and Tanya.

After messing around with them all for about four months and being caught up a couple of times, I chose Red to be my girlfriend. I must admit, she was a devil in disguise even though I now have a beautiful daughter and a handsome son by her.

One day while sitting in the alley in the project, three young ladies from the Jeffersons' projects came up to me. One of their names was Monica, Angel and tall Jane. Angel was real pretty, fine and attractive. The other two wasn't that hot or sexy to me or maybe they just wasn't my type. I talked with them for awhile.

This is where it all started concerning my drug case

The next day tall Jane seen me at the neighborhood store and told me, "My friend Angel like you."

I asked tall Jane, "Can she talk?"

She laughed and said, "Yes she can talk but she is shy."

A couple of days later, while standing on my sister's porch, Angel and her sister was passing by on their way to the neighborhood store when I yelled, "Angel, how are you doing?"

She stopped and said, "Oh, hi. How are you doing?"

"I'm ok. Where ya'll going?" I said.

She said, "We are headed to the store."

"Can I walk with ya'll?" I asked her.

The next day Angel came over to my sister house to see me. I invited her in and introduced her to my family. I can imagine what were going through Angel's mind as she sat in my sister house and listen at us talk to each other. All of my sisters and brothers was walking all around the house with tobacco in their mouth and spitting in soda cans. Angel didn't say anything to me about it but I know it had to cross her mind because if I were in her shoes, I probably would've asked her after we got outside.

A few days later Angel came by my sister house and asked me to walk over to the neighborhood community center. Once we got to the community center, Angel introduced me to her mother, who worked as a cook at the community center. Angel mother was very friendly and had a great sense of humor.

I really like Angel. She was very pretty and acted real mature. I never tried to have sex with Angel nor did I ever kiss her in a real sexual way. I must admit it crossed my mind several times, but I seen something in her that,, kept me from asking her. I really didn't know what it was at that time, but there was something different about Angel that set her apart from the other eight girls that I had messed with.

Nevertheless, I'm not sure but Angel probably bad mouthed me to her friends by telling them, "Girl, I can't believe he haven't kissed me in the mouth or asked me for no pussy. All he wants to do is smile at me, hold my hand and talk."

Angel looked so innocent but acted real mature.

My relationship with Angel shortly came to a ghost relationship based on my immaturity.

Now that Angel is gone, my relationship with Red have gotten serious.

Everyone in the John Hay Homes knew we were together. I was more serious about the relationship than Red was. There were other girls sweating me constantly but I was hung up on Red at the time.

A year later, Red was pregnant but lost the twins. Red mother, who worked in the coal mine asked us to come live with her for a while or until our apartment was ready.

It is now 1985, Red and I now have our own place and a beautiful daughter name Lynnikia. My daughter Lynnikia was my everything and everything was her to me.

My youth boys basketball team would steal my daughter every weekend. They would take Nikia shopping and everything else with them. They treated her like she was their little sister.

CHAPTER 3

JOBS AFTER JOBS

While volunteering at the neighborhood community center, I also worked a 5:00pm to closed shift at Popeye's Chicken. This Popeye's Chicken was in the hood on South Grand Avenue East.

There was this dope head girl named Leverna who was the closing manager.

She worked Wednesday through Sunday. Leverna loved smoking weed with cocaine.

Some people called them laced joints, premos or 51's.

Every night around 8:00pm, Leverna would ask us to let her know if we see another manager coming. We could smell the weed scent coming up out of the office, so we knew she was in there getting high. She would come out of the office with her eyes blood shot red, and ask us, "Is everything okay?"

We would all say, "It's kind of slow right now," but for real business was booming. Our reason for telling her that business was slow, because we was pocketing the money and stealing chicken, especially the raw chicken.

We would dump two full bus tubs of thighs and breasts into a large trash bag and dump ice on top of it. There would be about 300 pieces of chicken in the bag. We would also put two bags of spicy and mild seasoning in the bag. We would then sit the bag of chicken by the back door with the trash.

Once we went outside to dump the trash, we would throw the chicken in the trunk of Kenny's car. After the dishwasher was done cleaning the bus tubs, we would fill them back up with chicken before Leverna did her closing inventory.

Leverna would let us take most of the leftover chicken home with us, especially the wings, even though the left over legs, thighs and breasts was used for barbecue sandwiches; she didn't want a high left over chicken count.

As a manager, you never want a high left over count, especially as a closing manager because it shows your inability to control waste and manage an effective business.

Once Henry, Kenny and me got off work, we would go straight to the John Hay Homes project and open our own out of the trunk Popeye's Chicken. As we pulled up, there was niggas on every corner selling dope or shooting dice. Most of the niggas that was shooting dice was ballers. The niggas that was selling the dope was the baller's workers.

We would sell a leg, thigh, and a biscuit for $2.00 and a wing, breast and· a biscuit for $3.00. Keeping it real with you, we were selling the wing, breast and a biscuit for more than Popeye's was charging. A two piece white chicken, which is a wing and breast was only $2.49 at Popeye's but nobody ever complained to us.

As for the raw chicken, we only sold it in sixteen pieces for $15.00 in cash or $30.00 in food stamps. Most of the ballers would buy thirty two pieces each and give it to the girl who house they sold dope out of. We never ever had more than twenty pieces of raw chicken left over.

I would always tell Henry and Kenny to split the leftovers up between them and I would keep the seasoning for myself because my brothers who was selling dope would always have a barbecue cookout.

One day I went to work and there was a memo on the board over the time clock that said, "There will be a mandatory meeting tomorrow at 2: OOpm and all employees must be here." We asked Leverna what the meeting was going to be about but she had no idea.

The next day at the meeting, Earnest and Larry, who was the two main region managers spoke with us. Leverna didn't attend the meeting with us because she had to watch the store. Larry told us that, "someone is stealing and it must stop now."

Earnest then told us, "In sixty days, we are going to send some of ya'll out to the store on Chatman Road."

The Popeye's out on Chatman Road was way out by the mall which was about five miles from the house and all whites worked there.

Larry told us that they were going to put a camera on every cash register.

The following day, a young black youth threw a brick through the front window of the store. Leverna immediately called the police and reported the incident.

Once the police finally arrived, they asked Leverna did the camera over the register work. Leverna told the police that she didn't know whether the camera worked or not, but she will ask her supervisor tomorrow and she will give them a call tomorrow. I knew exactly who the youth was but I didn't say anything to the cops about him.

Leverna slipped up and told us that the cameras wasn't working. Henry, Kenny, and my eyes lit up like Christmas trees. That same night we was back up to our old hustling game.

After work, we headed to the project to open our out-of-trunk Popeye' business again.

As we drove up and was getting out of the car, one of the ballers named Stutter-Man asked us, "How . . . much do ya'll want for everything?"

I said, "Give us $500.00."

Stutter-Man told me, "That ain't no problem ni-ggas."

All I could do was burst out laughing. Stutter-Man reached in his pocket and pulled out a wad of money and gave me five crispy C-notes. I gave Henry and Kenny $180.00 each and took the $140.00 that was left. It was all profit for us because it didn't cost us a dime. But on the other hand, the rest of the ballers said, "L.J., you and your guys was out of order for that, more than Stutter-Man and his boys was hungry."

I said, "You are right, but we was just trying to get rid of it. I will keep what you said in mind."

A couple of days later, I got a job working for the Housing Authority since I was already volunteering at the community center. They hired me as a youth specialist.

One day while working at the community center, Red walked up and caught this girl named Angie sitting in between my legs on the gym bleachers. She asked me, "Who is this damn bitch?"

I said, "This is my friend Angie from Mississippi."

She then said, "You need to tell your so-called friend Angie to get up. I don't think your friend will be sitting in between your legs smiling like this bitch is doing."

Angie then said, "I'm not going to be too many more of your bitches. My name is Angie. A bitch is a female dog and I'm sure not a dog Mrs. Thang."

"Whatever bitch! You need to go find you a man because this one belongs to me," Red said.

"Red! you need to stop trippin' and go take my daughter home."

The next thing I knew, Red had stole on Angie. Angie jumped up and flew into Red. I immediately got up and broke them up for the simple reason they were at my job. I didn't want it to get back to my supervisor, Mrs. Kays, that I had two girls at my job fighting over me.

I then took Red into the community kitchen and told her, "It's no fun when the rabbit got the gun." In other words, I was telling her I don't say nothing when you are with your friends. "And don't forget we are only together for the sake of my daughter."

Red then told me, "Fuck you! My baby and me don't need you. We can make it without you. So you can have that stinkin' bitch."

I said, "I bet you can! Take my damn baby home."

She then walked back into the gym and told her sister Pam to come on. I then went back into the gym and told Angie to follow me into the office. I then said, "Angie, I am so sorry. I promise you that nothing else would happen like this again."

About four months later, Red caught an attempted murder charge in which she stabbed a guy several times for grabbing on her after she refused to talk to him. Therefore, I had to go over Red mother's house to get my daughter. I went down to the courthouse, and the court gave me custody of Lynnikia.

My sister Annie would babysit for me while I went to work. Once I got off work, I would pick Lynnikia up from Annie's house and take her over Angie's house with me. Angie welcomed my daughter with open arms. She also had a young baby of her own that I loved like she was my own.

My relationship with Angie became real serious for about six months. Angie had a heart of gold and her mother and sister took advantage of her all the time. Angie mother and sister really didn't like me because I put her up on their game. I wouldn't allow Angie to lend them money or food stamps. I would keep all of Angie's money and food stamps with me.

After awhile, Angie's mother and sister began to get in her ear by telling her that she was crazy for watching my daughter for me while I ran the streets. I could tell that Angie mother and sister was trying to use her watching my daughter to break us up. So one day I told Angie, "Angie you don't have to watch my daughter. I will drop her off at my sister whenever I go to work or hit the streets.

She said, "I don't have no problem with watching your daughter. I was just telling you what my mother and sister was saying."

"Angie, you need to tell your people to mind their business and stay out of your business." Shortly after the conversation between Angie and I, we broke-up because I can't stand a woman who lets her mother or any other family member run her house or stay in her business. Some people may feel that my reason for leaving Angie was crazy and that's okay with me.

One day as I walked into the office at work, my co-workers said, "L.J., guess what? We are going to Memphis in a couple of weeks."

"What are we going to Memphis to do?" I asked them. They told me that the Memphis Housing Authority Recreation Department called and invited us to come play in their youth basketball tournament. My guy Bucky told me that he had already made us reservations at a nice hotel in a good location.

After leaving Springfield, Illinois on a Friday around 6:00pm, we arrived in Memphis, Tennessee around 1:00am in the morning. There was the three of us, two adult women, six teenager girl cheerleaders and fifteen teenager boys that made the trip.

As we pulled up into the hotel parking lot, there was prostitutes standing on both ends of the hotel parking lot. As the young boys got out of the vans, they immediately whispered at the prostitutes and they came running up to the vans. I said, "Excuse me, these are young boys and we are in town to play in a youth basketball tournament at the Orange Mound Community Center."

One of the prostitutes said, "We can serve them too."

We laughed and then I said, "We are good. We must check-in and get to bed."

Once we got upstairs to the rooms, we splitted the youth up among us. The two women took three girls each. Bucky, Reggie and myself took five boys each.

As we got up that morning for breakfast, I overheard a couple of players talking about they got into a fight last night. I thought they was talking about a fight between each other. I didn't know that they had got into a fight with the prostitute pimps until we was headed down the stairs to the vans to go play a 10:00am game. As we was going down the stairs, the four pimps was coming up the stairs. Just as they passed me, the food that they had in their hand came flying back down the stairs. As I turned and looked, the pimps and my players was fighting. I dropped my bag and ran back up the stairs to help my players. One of the pimps pulled out a gun and said, "Back up niggers" and shot up in the air a couple of times. We then came down the stairs and two of the pimps tried to rush a couple of the players again.

Once again the fight was on.

This time, the pimp that had the gun pulled out his gun and shot one of my players in the arm and shot at another player in which the bullet went straight through his jacket under his right arm. After seeing and hearing that they had shot one of the players, the pimps jumped into a Blazer truck and took off. I quickly wrapped the player arm up and rushed him to the hospital.

Once I got the player to the hospital, I immediately called his mother and told her that he had been shot. The player's mother called me some of everything that you could possibly think of and told me to bring her "damn son home right now." All I could do were say "yes mam" to her.

I must keep it real with you, we finished the other two games before we headed back to the crib.

A couple of days after we returned back home from Memphis, our supervisor called us into her office and fired us for insubordination. Even though I knew that my co-workers left their youth unsupervised, I told our supervisor that I did what policy required us to do.

She then said, "You. guys should have picked a better hotel in a better location. That's it. You guys can come get your check on the fifteenth at 2:00pm. Oh yea, you guys may appeal my decision."

We then walked out of her office. Once we got outside, I told my coworkers, "You guys owe me a favor. The young ladies got to keep their job.

After appealing Mrs. Kay's decision, all three of us was hired back. The reason that we won the appeal was because the youth and their parents spoke up for us and told them that it really wasn't our fault. The youth told their parents that they sneaked out while we was sleep.

About three months later, I got another job working as a manager at Take Care of Business Kitchen. After being open for only one year, the owner asked me to buy the business with everything in it for $14,000.

Now that I look back, I was a fool for not buying that kitchen. There's no doubt in my mind I would have been successful in that business. Maybe I wouldn't be here sitting in federal prison writing my life story. But on the other hand, I believe in the old saying, "Everything happens for a reason."

After Take Care of Business Kitchen closed down, I became self-employed. I became a so-called pimp. This business went against all of my beliefs and promises that I made to myself as a youth.

CHAPTER 4

SELF BROKEN PROMISES

As a teenager I made myself a few promises. I promised myself that whenever I had children, they would all be by the same woman and she would become Mrs. Joiner. Guess what? I have six beautiful children by four different women. I have two beautiful daughters and four handsome sons.

I now know that there is nothing cool or good about having children by different women. The only thing that come with it is baby-mama drama. Now baby-mama drama is a conflict or contrast of character between two or more women about the baby's dad.

The sad thing about my baby-mama drama my children suffer the most. First of all, my children are separated from each other. They really don't know each other, they just know of each other. There is a big difference between knowing of someone and actually knowing them. The baby-mama drama was so focussed around me that my children's well-being was put on the back burner.

The baby-mama drama come about because the women have a desire by nature to fulfill their role in a relationship in the appropriate order. We as men cause this unwarranted drama due to our sexual desire and immaturity to only desire one mate.

The baby-mama conflict is caused when we as men do not commit to them in a monogamous relationship. Women desire to be the one and only true love.

When they do not receive it, they release their frustration in the form of anger and disrespect toward the man and the other woman. Sometimes the women even begin to hate the man's other children by the other women. In the heat of chaotic baby-mama drama, the women forget that the children are innocent.

As I look back into my baby-mama drama relationships, I must first think of my state of mind at that time. During this time, it was all about L.J. and what he wanted. I failed to understand that a relationship is like a bank account . . . You can only withdraw what you deposit into the account. I must admit that I did not deposit anything positive into any of the relationships with my children mother. So how can I expect to withdraw anything positive out of them?

I take full responsibility for my baby-mama drama and the impact it has had on my children. There's not a day or night that comes and goes that I don't pray for my children. I also pray for the mothers of my children, that they would put their feelings for me aside and focus on my children getting to know each other while I am serving this time in prison.

I also promised myself that if any man ever tried to pimp one of my sisters or my daughters, I would kill him. Guess what? One day while I was sitting on the hood of my car a prostitute walked up to me and said, "What's up L. J.? I've been watching your country ass for a long time. I'm really feeling you. How would you like to be my pimp?" I replied, "Excuse me. Did you say what I thought you said? I'm not with that. You might want to check with one of my older brothers, that's their thing." She then said, "If you never tried it, how do you know that it's not your thing? I tell you what Sweetie, I live at 2109 Lawrence Street. Swing by later and I will change your mind." My response was, "I don't think you can do that." As she got ready to walk off, she told me to call her Break-A-Nigga. I said, "You got that, Break-A-Nigga."

Around 8:00 p.m., I jumped in my car and went to see what was up with Break-A-Nigga. As I got out of my car and walked up to the door and knocked, Break-A-Nigga answered the door with nothing on. I couldn't believe that she didn't tell me to hold on until she went and put some clothes on or something. She just told me to come in and have a seat while she took a bath.

On her way to the bathtub she stopped and bent over right in front of me. All I could do was say—my, my, my, how can one woman have all of that. She was fine as she could be and had a very sexy walk.

As she got out of the tub, she came back into the living room and asked me to dry her off. I paused for maybe ten seconds before taking the towel out of her hand. She then told me you don't have to be nervous or afraid, because I want bite you." Now, while drying her off, she grabbed my hands and put them around her waist, then asked me . . . "What can I do for you to make you my pimp?" I just smiled at her. We then went into her bedroom and sat on her bed. Believe it or not, I grabbed her by her chin and stared at her for about five minutes. Then I asked her why wasn't she a model or a teacher? She looked me straight in my face and said, "This is all that I know how to do.

I dropped out of school because I got pregnant at the age of fourteen and my parents put me out of the house." I replied, "How are you?" She told me that she was twenty years old, so I told her my age, which was twenty-five. I really didn't like calling her Break-A-Nigga, so I asked her, "What's your real name?" She told me that her name was Marie, but asked me not to call her Marie in public. I must say that I felt sorry for her, so I began to speak positive and encouraging things to her. "Look Marie, you have your whole life ahead of you. You're pretty and you're smart. You can still be who and whatever you desire to be. I will help you get your life back on track," I said. She then told me, "No one wants me. I have been walked over and stumped on."

"Marie, that's not true," I said. The next thing that I knew she was undressing me. Then she gave me oral sex. I tried to stop this girl at first, but I fell weak. Before I knew it she grabbed a condom and put it on me and rode me like I was a horse. Once she got finished riding me, she went into the bathroom and grabbed a towel, then washed me up. Then she took me into her bathroom and asked me to keep her company while she took a shower.

While she was in the shower, a couple of prostitutes that I knew through my baby-mom came over. They had a key to the house, so they were standing in the living room when we came out of the bathroom together. As the both of them saw me they said, "I know this is not Red's stuck-up man, L.J." I must admit, I was so ashamed that those prostitutes saw me at Marie's house, or should I say Break-A-Nigga's house. Both of the prostitutes had tried to get me to turn a trick with them and one of them use to hang out with my sister back in the day.

As Break-A-Nigga got ready to introduce me to the prostitutes, I told her that I knew both of them from around the way. Then she told them, to my surprise, "This is our new daddy. Do you whores have a problem with it? I didn't think so. If he tell you whores to jump, you better say—how high, daddy?" So I told Marie to step outside with me. Once we got outside I said, "You are very bold and straight forward. "I'm not bold, I'm just serious about what I want," she replied. Then she grabbed me by the hand. "I like your cute little ass and I'm going to teach you the game," she said.

"So, are you just going to make me your pimp," I asked?

"Yes, I am," she said. "Now please come by around 7: 00 so I can give you the game before me and those whores go to the track to get you your money."

I let her know that I understood. I hopped back into my car and headed back to the projects.

Once I got back to the John Hay Homes, everybody was asking me where in the world have I been? I told them that I just went for a ride. My brother J.W. then told me that a young lady named Kathy had been looking for me. Kathy was married, so I picked my time with her carefully.

The next day I went back over to Break-A-Nigga' house. She did just as she had said . . . she gave me the game! She told me that I must sample my product to make sure it would sell and make me money. Therefore, I made Tina and Ms. Good-Head both give me oral sex and sex. They both passed the test with flying colors. Marie told me that she would make sure that our money was straight at all times and she would make sure that they took care of themselves all around.

She also taught me how to be a watchman for them while they were working. If they got into a vehicle I had to write down the license plate number just in case they didn't return in fifteen minutes. I also had to make sure that the other pimps didn't rob them. Another one of my duties was to help watch out for the (po-po) police. This was a tough job for me, plus I really didn't have the cold heart that the job required.

There would be nights when Break-A-Nigga and the other two prostitutes would bring thousands of dollars home with credit cards and check books. While turning tricks with the customers, they would rob them as well. I never went shopping with those prostitutes, so I don't know how they were getting away with using stolen credit cards and checks. All I know is that they were doing it and I can't ever recall them getting caught.

About six months later, I gave the pimping game up. One day I went by Break-A-Nigga's crib and called her and my other two whores into the living room and told them that I was hanging up my pimping jersey. I apologized to them for disrespecting them and having them to sell their precious bodies for me. "You all are so beautiful," I said. "You don't have to be a prostitute.

Your dreams are still alive, so you can still be whatever you desire to be.

You all still have your whole lives ahead of you. You are queens and deserve the utmost respect and love." While I was talking to them, tears poured from their eyes.

"We're going to miss all of the good meals you cook for us, especially on Sunday," said Ms. Good-Head. Tina had something to say as well.

"You really treated us with so much respect, especially with us being prostitutes and all."

"Believe it or not I never seen you all as prostitutes. I see you as confused queens. Marie, what's up Sweetheart? I can't keep on pretending to be someone who I'm not and disrespecting you all. I care about you beautiful sisters." Marie didn't want to let go that easy'.

"If you loved us, you wouldn't leave us?" said Marie.

"Baby girl listen to me, I am only leaving because I care about you all and I can't continue to misuse you all. We can still be friends and I will still come by every now and then to make you all a meal and kick it with you sweet ladies."

Even though I apologized to Marie, Tina and Ms. Good-Head, who finally told me that her name was Rosline, they never truly forgave me for hanging up my pimping jersey. That was okay with me, because I was no longer mistreating them and my conscience was clear of it.

The last promise that I made myself as a teenager was that I would never mess a round with a married woman. Guess what? I broke that promise as well.

One day while standing on the corner of 15th street in the John Hay Homes Project kicking it with my brother Cheek, two beautiful young ladies walked up to us and asked us did we have any weed. I politely asked them where they where from.

One of them was from Mound Bayou, Mississippi and the other one was from St. Louis Missouri. My brother, Cheek really couldn't talk with them because his baby-mom was also standing out there with us. Once I walked them to their car right before they got in, they told me their names. One was named Denise, and the other one's name was Kathy. Both of the females worked at St. John Hospital.

After about two months of seeing Kathy, I remembered that I had met her at Popeyey's chicken previously with her sister-n-law, not knowing that she was married to Christine's brother. One night Kathy and Denise came by the project to cop their usual dime bag of weed from Cheek, but he was 86, which meant he was out of product. I then asked Kathy could I talk to her for a second.

Her response was, "sure you can."

"Do you think I can call you or come by sometimes," I asked?

"How are you going to call me or come by? You don't have my number or address. So I guess you're trying to ask me for my seven digits on the slick tip?"

"I guess you can say that," I replied. Then she gave me her number.

A couple of days later I gave Kathy a call. We talked on the phone for about a half-hour. She told me that she thought that I wasn't for real. Before hanging up the phone, she gave me her sister's address for whatever reason and told me to come by the next day at around five o'clock. As we got off the phone, I said to myself that she must have a boyfriend living with her.

The next day I went to meet Kathy at her sister's house. I refused to get out of my car and go knock on the door because I thought maybe she didn't want nobody to see me for whatever reason. So I just blew my horn and she came to the door. She told me to hold on for a minute and she'd be right out. A few minutes later, she came out of the house and got into my car.

"Can we go somewhere and talk for a while," I asked her?

"Sure," she said. "I am with you as long as we don't go to Garden Court. "I tell you what, we will go to the Holiday Inn out on Sixth Street.

As we got to the hotel and went into the room, I noticed that Kathy was nervous. I tried to ease her mind by just letting her know that I wouldn't harm her.

"Kathy, is something wrong? I'm not a rapist nor do I bite, so you have nothing to worry about."

Her response was, "I promise you that none of those are the reasons that I am nervous."

"What is it," I asked? She just looked at me and smiled. Then she told me that she wanted to ask me a personal question. "You can ask me whatever you want to know about me and I will be truthful with you."

"!i\.re you married or do you have a girlfriend," she asked?

"Believe it or not, I am not married and I don't have a girlfriend."

You would think that I would have asked her the same questions, but I didn't.

That night the only thing that Kathy and I did was watch "The Hand That Rock The Cradle" and ate pizza. After watching the movie, I dropped Kathy off.

Before she went into the house, we made plans to hook up again.

About three days later, I went to grab Kathy again. This time since I already had a room at the Red Roof Inn, I took Kathy there. Even though I didn't drink, I had some gin, beer, and wine coolers in the room. So I asked Kathy would she like something to drink.

"Sure," she said. "I would like some gin if you have any." I figured she must want some gin to make her sin. I didn't have orange juice, so I told her to stay in the room and I would be right back. I hopped into my car and drove up the street to Shop-N-Save, where I grabbed a quart of orange juice.

When I returned to the hotel room with the orange juice, I saw that Kathy had gotten very comfortable. She was sitting in the bed with her silky red panties and braw on when I got back. Excuse me I said as I placed my hand over my eye. "I'm sorry."

She then said, "Stop trippin' and come here." As I got closer to her, I could smell the gin on her breath.

"Would you like some orange juice with your gin," I offered?

"No, not now baby," she said. "I want some of you right now." As I sat on the bed she immediately started rubbing and kissing on me. Then she took my shirt off of me and pushed me back on the bed. She then got on top of me and began grinding on me. The next thing I knew, we were getting busy.

Once we were done and woke up, we took a bath together. After we got dressed I asked Kathy the question that I should have asked her the first time that we went to the hotel. "Are you married or do you have a boyfriend?"

As I stated earlier, I thought that she had a boyfriend since she had given me her sister's address instead of her address. It turned out that she didn't have a boyfriend, but even worse, she was married! "You got to be joking with me."

"No, I'm not joking. I'm married," she said. Then she showed me her ring on her finger. I never paid any attention to her hand. Then she said, "You never asked me, but I apologize for not telling you. But on the other hand, things are not good at home between me and my husband. We're talking about getting a divorce." Now I found myself apologizing to Kathy for making her commit adultery. Even though we apologized to each other for our actions, we continued our affair. We became secret lovers.

One day, Kathy and I went to St. Louis to the mall and grabbed us a couple of nice outfits. After shopping and enjoying a nice steak and potatoe dinner, we returned back to Springfield. Once we got back, I dropped Kathy off at home. Then I decided to go go by my sister Annies's house. As I walked into Annie's house, my sweet daughter Lynnikia came running to me. I picked her up and gave her a kiss on the cheek. After putting her back down I gave her five dollars. Everyone kept asking me where I had been for the past couple of weeks. I told them that I had been just chillin' and that I was good. A few minutes later my sister, Black said, "L.J., Red is out there breaking all of your windows out of your car." I ran outside and sure enough she had broke all of my windows out and had cut a hole in the driver's side door. I ran up to her and snatched the axe out of her hand. I know now that I could have gotten hurt, but I wasn't thinking at the time. I grabbed her and slapped her a couple of times and pushed her against the car with my hand around her neck. My sisters grabbed me, yelling and screaming, "L. J. don't you hurt this girl."

"Well you all better get this damn fool before I kill her," I spoke out of anger. Then I threw her to the ground. As I turned around to go into the house to call the police so that I could get a report to show the rental place, my daughter was standing there looking. I felt so bad that my daughter had seen me put my hands on her mother. I grabbed my daughter and went into the house to call the police. A few minutes later the police drove up and asked me what happened to my car. Red tried to tell the police that I had jumped on her, but the female officer that knew me asked her . . .

"Did you do this to his car?" Red didn't answer her, so she addressed me. "Do you want to press charges against her?"

"No," I replied. "I'll be okay." After the police left, I had my guy, B.D. report the accident, or should I say the incident. Once we got to the airport and I told them what happened to their car, they told me that they needed five hundred dollars for the deductible before they could take the car back, because I hadn't taken out insurance on the car. I reached into my pocket and gave them the five hundred dollars.

"Mr. Joiner, we appreciate your business said the supervisor but you can never rent another car from our agency.

"Okay, I'm sorry.". Budget Rental car passed my name around to the other car rental agencies. Therefore, I wasn't able to rent a car from any of the rental agencies at the airport.

In between time things had gotten a little more serious between Kathy and Me. One night I went over to Kathy's house and she talked me into spending the night. I must admit that I knew I was breaking the rule of thumb by staying at Kathy's crib, being that I knew she was married. Yea, you don't have to say it, I know that I was playing Russian Roulette with my life. Nevertheless, Kathy and I enjoyed our night together. We watched porno flicks and once again we got busy in her big water bed. While we were getting busy, Kathy told me, "L. J. I really don't know how to tell you this, but I am beginning to have feelings for you."

So my response was, "Dig this, you must be psychic, because I'm feeling the same way."

"I'm for real," she told me. "You make me feel special and loved." How could something so wrong feel so right?

"Kathy, the ball is in your court. You must work your marriage out which ever way the wind blows and we will go from there. One thing for sure, Sweetheart, we can't keep being secret lovers forever." Tears begin to formed in the well of her eyes.

"L.J., I don't want my husband anymore, I want you." Said Kathy.

"That's cool, but you still have to settle things with him before we can move on with our relationship." Then she had a question for me . . .

"L.J., can you give me some time to work it out with Mike before you give up on me?"

"Sure, I'll give you as much time as you need, but just keep it real with me and I will respect whatever decision you make.

In the meantime and between time, my baby-mom, Red found out about Kathy somehow. One night she went to Kathy's house and knocked on her door to confront her concerning me. Kathy told me that Red told her she had better leave me alone. Kathy responded by telling Red, "He told me that he's a free man, so you must be confused. I don't even know you. So how did you get my address?" Red's reply was that she had followed us one night.

After Red and Kathy had their little talk, Red broke her front window out. Then a couple of days later, Red told Kathy's husband that Kathy was cheating on him with me. Even though Kathy's husband knew who I was, he never confronted me about her. I guess Red ran Kathy off, because I never heard anything else from her nor did I ever see her again. I now know that the old saying is true . . . "Promises are made to be broken," because I broke all of myself promises that I had made as a teenager.

CHAPTER 5

A GAME WITH TWO CHOICES

Life is all about choices from the womb to the tomb. Guess what? None of us are exempt from making a bad choice or two in life. I once heard a man say—"To every choice there's a consequence, and to every action, there's a reaction."

After working job after job, and seeming to be getting nowhere, I decided to play a game with two choices . . . death or prison. I made the decision to join my family's drug business in which they were selling gunpowder weed. They sold nick's, dimes, and twenties. They also sold ounces for eighty dollars.

My father started me off working in the house as a cutter and packer.

After learning the game, how to weigh the weed, bag it and count the money, I began to work the street corner. Every morning I would get up and go down to the family drug house to work. They would give me fifteen bags which consisted of five nickel bags, five dimes, and five twenties. They would give me one of each every time I sold out. I was given ten dollars for every ounce that I came to the house to purchase for a customer. The ounces were so fat, we would take about a dime bag *out* before we gave it to the customers." None of the customers ever complained about the size of the ounces. I would stand *out* on the corner from eight a. m. to twelve midnight. The only time that I left the corner was to go and grab a bite to eat. Before leaving to get something to eat, I would give my package to one of my family members to hold, or I would hide it. I would always make sure that nobody was looking before I hid my drugs. Once I got back, I would waste no time getting back on my hustle.

There would be some days where I would make one hundred and fifty dollars, and other days I would only make sixty dollars. However, on the first and fifteenth of each month, it would look like we were giving away free government cheese. I would make about five hundred dollars on both days.

As time passed, I began to travel to pick up several pounds of marijuana from the family's connection. It was only an eight mile round trip. My brothers taught me how to be a bud runner. They told me to never panic when I see the big-hat boys. That's another word for the cops. And they told me to never hit my brakes. They also told me to never be afraid to pass them on the highway.

We always made sure that the vehicle; whether car, van, or truck had proper registration, insurance, and the individuals had valid drivers' license. Oh yea, I would receive one hundred dollars for every trip that I made. I now know that it wasn't luck that I never got stopped going or coming with the weed, God was just watching over me. Nevertheless, because of my blindness, I took my hustling game to the next level.

Even though the family weed business was treating me good, I went and got a job working at the Hilton Hotel. I must keep it real with you, I only took the job as a cover up. While workin at the hotel, my weed business took off like a jet. I was serving all of the maids and housemen. After a week or so, I hooked up with a young white maid named Trisha. Now Trisha would sell my weed for me to the guest in the hotel. She was also a prostitute. She would turn tricks with the male guests while cleaning their rooms. I would take care of Trisha for selling the bud for me. Every pay day after the maids went and cashed their checks around the corner at the bank, I would meet them down in the basement of the hotel to collect my money. Some of them would owe me as much as a hundred bucks.

Once I got my bankroll together I bought my own eighth of an ounce of skunk bud from my father. After I sold the eighth of an ounce, I purchased a quarter kilo. I sold the whole quarter kilo in dime bags. Then I bought a half a kilo and bagged it up in dimes and twenties. After saving my money, I bought,, my first car, which was a sky blue 1977 Monte Carlo. I gave an old lady five hundred dollars for it. I immediately had a junkie to go and steal me a sound system and he installed it for me. I have him an eighth of my skunk bud for the system. I remember jumping into my ride and going to Auto Zone. I hooked it up with some floor mats, cleaning supplies, seat covers, air freshener and a white steering wheel wrap. I rode by the carwash and gave my ride a thorough cleaning.

With my car looking fresh and clean, I rolled across town to the John Hay Homes Project, where my family and all the homies and dealers hung out. As I got out of my Monte Carlo, my brothers and nephew said—"Look at Woo Daddy, got him a nice ride. Boy the game is good to you." I had to try and keep up with the rest of the Joiners. Now that my weed business was booming, my family called a meeting and told us that they had a drug that would sell better and faster. It was called powder cocaine. After my older brothers gave us the game on how to bag up the cocaine and sell it, we got busy. We sold twenties (twenty bucks), sixteenths (one hundred bucks), eight balls (one hundred and fifty bucks), quarter ounces (Four hundred bucks), half ounces (six hundred bucks), and ounces (twelve hundred bucks). As the drug changed we had to increase our security. The police began to roll through the project more often and the stick up boys came out of nowhere. To make a long story short, the cocaine increased the violence.

Most of the old players, pimps, hustlers, and prostitutes would shoot the cocaine with heroin mixed in. They called it "Speed balling." The rest of them would just snort the cocaine. The young people in my neighborhood during this time either snorted the cocaine or smoked it mixed with weed. Some people called these joints "primos" or "lace joints" while others called them "cool fifty one's."

One day my brother, Pop, stopped by the block and told us, "I forgot to tell you guys to never get high off your own supply!' Come to find out, Pop was talking from experience. All of the older brothers were getting high in some form or fashion, except B.C. This is the point in my life when my image began to be created. Being in the drug business gave me power and fame. It also gave me a reputation that I really didn't need. While in the game, I became three people in one. I became who my posse and costumers built me up to be; then I was the person I thought I was at the time; and I became a confused person struggling to regain my true identity of my true self. As each day passed, my so called image-man became stronger and dominant because I was feeding him through my actions. Other people helped in feeding this monster of a man. Therefore, since the image-man was being fed the most, he slowly took control of me.

Not to get too religious on you, but I am a firm believer that God gives us warning signs as we travel through this journey of life. About four months after we switched from selling weed to selling cocaine, I got caught in a raid at my father's house. The police found cocaine, weed, two hand guns, two thousand dollars worth of food stamps, and fourteen hundred in cash. My father and four other family members were arrested with me. We were charged and indicted for conspiracy to sell cocaine. At trial, I was found guilty of being in a disorderly house and was sentenced to a year on probation.

As we got ready to enter 1990, the family and I decided to throw a big New Year's Eve party. We rented a large building that was formerly a funeral home. The place still had caskets down in the basement, so we only used the top floor and the second floor. There arcade games on the first floor, and the dance floor was on the second floor. We charged five dollars admission at the door. All of the drinks were free and everybody was given a fat joint of skunk weed upon entering the party. In order to keep them from doubling,, back for the free marijuana, we stamped their hands with our logo which was the letter 'J' with a dollar sign in it—$.

My family and I decided that we didn't need to hire any security because we had about twenty family members involved. My brother, Bob, two of my nephews, and two girlfriends of my other brothers collected the money at the door.

There was about six of us posted on each floor to keep order, making sure that no fights or anything jumped off. We had advertised heavily by posting flyers everywhere, so the place was packed and the party was jumping. All of the gold digging women was there wearing their sexy new outfits, which they had bought from the mall with their public aid checks, better known as welfare checks. The term gold digger in the hood is a woman or women who is seeking a dope-man or an individual for financial and material gain. Since the gold diggers were present, my girl Rena watched me like a hawk. About two hours into the party I noticed people were running downstairs hollering—"he got a gun!" I immediately ran up the stairs to see what was going on. There I saw a guy holding a gun on my brother named Head. The guy had it pointed directly in his face. Now I had just finished talking with the guy's brother, Steve.

Steve brother then looked at me and said, "This nigga is trippin' because I slapped my bitch." I proceeded to ask him to leave but he didn't. Meanwhile, Steve came up the stairs. Once he talked with his brother, Steve came up to me and said, "L.J. I'm going to get my brother and we're going to leave. I don't want any problems with you and your family."

So Steve grabbed his brother and they left. They were members of the well known Vice Lords Street Gang.

After Steve and his brother left, we told all of the party attendants that everything was cool. My brother Bob and Tane told me what had caused the problem. They told me that Steve brother came to the door and asked could he come in for a minute and holler at his brother. My brother, Cheek's girlfriend told him no, but my nephew, Randy told him to pay the five bucks and if he came back within fifteen minutes, he could get his money back. Bob then told me that Steve brother asked Cheek's girlfriend could he holler at her for a minute. Her reply was, "hell no" So the fool walked up on her and slapped her. As they rushed him, that's when he pulled out the gun. Once my brother, Cheek got back to the party, his girlfriend and a few of his buddies told him what had happened. We tried to stop Cheek from seeking immediate revenge. Instead, we told his to wait until after the party was over, but he said, "fuck that, I'm going to go and kill that nigga and whoever else that want some." He jumped into his clean Bonnevile and took off with about four of his guys. Once Cheek and his guys returned to the party, he told us that he had seen him. "Yea, I seen that nigga at the Ho Ho's and he took off running. I shot at the nigga about six times. I don't know whether I hit the nigga or not." My brother, Tane and I told Cheek to chill out and we would go and see what's up tomorrow.

About an hour later, Steve, his brother, and several other Vice Lord's busted into the party with their guns waving. As I was coming out of the restroom, I heard Steve brother saying, "where is that nigga Cheek? I'm going to kill that nigga." While he was looking for Cheek, I saw Cheek slipping out of the door. A few minutes later Steve's brother looked me right in the face, but one of the other Vice Lord's called him, "hey dog, that nigga must not be in here." In the meantime I was trying to get over by the couch where our guns were. As I got down and crawled over to the couch, my brother, Rob was already grabbing the guns. As we raised up, several gun shots were being fired. I then looked to me left and seen Ike lying on the floor. We immediately started shooting at the Vice Lords. There were people running and screaming everywhere. Between us and them, there was so many shots fired in that place that I couldn't believe that nobody got shot, or at least that I knew of.

In between time, a couple of guys had rushed Ike to the hospital where he was pronounced dead. A couple of days later there was rumors going around that Cheek girlfriend was messing around with Dawg. There were also rumors that Cheek used Ike as a shield that night since Dawg came back to the party looking for Cheek to kill him. This rumor about Cheek supposedly using Ike as a shield almost ended a long lasting family friendship between us and Mr. D's family. Ike is was the son of Mr. D. who we lived with when our homes were destroyed years back by the Christmas fire and the tornado. About a week after Ike's funeral, we were gathered at my father's spot and heard somebody banging on the back door as if they were the raid task force. We quickly grabbed our heat and ran to both doors. As I peeped out of the window, I shouted, "It's the police man!" Before they could knock the door down, we had put the guns into the trap pocket that we had built inside one of the sofa in the house.

The reason that we ran to both of the doors with our guns is because we thought it was the Vice Lords trying to creep up on us. The cops came in shouting, "this is a raid! Everybody down on the floor now, and put your hands behind your back!" They all had on mask, making for a scary scene. After we got down on the floor we were all placed in handcuffs.

While lying on the floor, I seen one of the police reach into the vent and come out with about a quarter pound of weed and a few boxes of sandwich baggies. As the police helped us off of the floor, they took the cuffs off of everyone except me, my brother Kid, and a prostitute named Hot Pepper.

Then they placed us three and my father under arrest.

Once we got down to the county jail and booked in, we were told what we were being charged with. The female officer told the prostitute that she had an outstanding warrant for prostitution. My father was arrested because it was his house. My brother, Kid was arrested because he was on probation and in a disorderly house. As the officer got to me, he told me that I was arrested for a drug sell. I asked him, "who did I sell some drugs to? I don't sell no drugs. I work at Wendy's."

"So how did you end up with the one hundred dollars that we sent into the house by our informant to purchase cocaine," he asked me?

"I gave someone change for it." I could tell that the agent really didn't believe me. The one thing that I had in my favor was that I worked at Wendy's at the time. A few minutes later, after the agent finished talking to me, one of the guards that worked at the jail came and took me upstairs to 'J Block'.

All of the dudes in the cell block were sleep.

That morning my cell mate tapped my bed and asked me did I want to eat breakfast. At around 10 a.m. I got up and washed my face and brushed my chops.

As I came out of the cell, the first person I saw was Dawg, Steve's brother from the New Year's Eve Party. Dawg immediately got up and walked into his cell. I knew mostly everyone that was in 'J Block'. Most of them were homies from the John Hay Homes. Moments later Dawg came back out into the day room area. We kept looking at each other, but never said a word to each other.

My cell mate walked out to the day room area and looked at me and said, "L.J., what are you doing here?"

"What's up C.B.? How long have you been in here," I asked? "Why didn't you call Rena so I could come and bond you out?"

"Man I'm on the way to Joliet." Then we got up and went into the cell.

That's when C.B. gave me his info and asked me to look out for him. I gave him my word that I would look out for him. I gave him the 411 about Dawg and the whole situation. That was all it took for C.B. to be ready to go to war.

"Do you want me to go and smash that nigga for you?"

"No," I replied. "C.B.! C.B.! Hold on, let me go holler at him first."

After we finished eating lunch, Dawg came over to my cell and asked to speak with me for a second. I said sure, and asked C.B. to step out of the cell.

As Dawg entered the cell he placed two fingers on his right hand over his heart, which meant he came in peace.

"L.J., I'm sorry about what happened to your homie, Ike. I didn't shoot him."

"Check this out Dawg, I don't know whether you shot him or not, but you know the word on the street is that you did it."

"L.J. believe me, I didn't do it. This is why I turned myself in, so I wouldn't get into a shoot-out with y'all. I knew y'all were coming after us."

"Yea, we were also thinking that y'all was going to creep up on us," I said. As I looked out into the day room area, I noticed all of the guys looking at us. Dawg told me that the reason that he slapped Cheek's girlfriend was because she disrespect him after he told her that he didn't want her the day before the party, then she tried to front on him at the party. We talked for about five more minutes then shook hands.

The next day around 11 a.m. Ike's brother, Rich came into 'J Block' on a traffic violation. I immediately went over to talk with Rich. I informed him that Dawg was on the block and that we had talked. Rich quickly jumped up and ran over to confront Dawg about shooting his brother. I ran and jumped in between them. In came the Doom Squad, busting through the doors yelling, "Do we have a problem here?" We all said no sir. A few minutes later a guard called me to the window and asked me what was going on. I told him that it was just a misunderstanding and we were okay.

The next day, I was told to bunk and junk, which meant I was leaving.

About fifteen minutes later, a guard came through the door and said, "Joiner, let's go." I ran to Rich's cell and gave him a hug and told him to stay cool.

I also stopped by Dawg's cell and told him to chill and keep his head up. As I got downstairs, I was released on my own recognizance. In other words, that meant that I promised to appear for my court date or I would forfeit the eight hundred and fifty dollars that the police had taken from me during the raid.

Since I was released, I don't know what became of Rich and Dawg's issue. Even though I seen Rich after he got out, we never talked about the issue. A couple of weeks after I was released, I got a letter from the court saying that no charges were being filed against me. There was also a check with the letter for seven hundred and fifty dollars. I guess they kept the hundred bucks from the drug sell. I didn't bother to ask them about it either. About six months after being released from the county jail, my father died in prison. He was already sick from years of heavy drinking.

CHAPTER 6

L.J.'S CRACK WORLD

Once again, just as my business started back booming, a new and improved drug came on the scene called crack cocaine. Some peopled called this new mind altering monster crack, or crack rock, while others called it ready rock. A couple of brothers came down from the twin cities and showed Me and Cheek how to cook crack, and how the business worked. There names were Kevin and Nelson.

The first thing that we did was, we went and bought some cooking supplies.

After leaving Big Lot's, we stopped by Shop and Save where we grabbed some ice, baking soda, and sandwich bags. Then we headed over to the stash house.

Once we made it to the stash house, we quickly jumped out of the car and ran into the house and locked the door just in case the stick-up boys were creeping.

After getting situated, Kevin and Nelson asked me for the powder cocaine.

I went into the back bedroom and returned with a quarter kilo of crystal powder cocaine, which was nine ounces. Kevin weighed out each ounce of cocaine and said to me, "L.J., you guys got two hundred and fifty two grams here."

Then he weighed out six ounces of baking soda and combined it with the cocaine in the large cake bowl. Nelson had made his way over to the stove and he had a large glass pot about half full with boiling water.

Kevin, bring the cocaine mix, said Nelson. i'm coming," replied Kevin. I'm just trying to make sure that I mixed it real good." Nelson turned the stove from high, down to low, then he added the cocaine and baking soda mixture into the pot of boiling water. It wasn't long before he turned the stove off and began shaking the glass pot for a couple of minutes.

"We got white jello, guys," said Nelson. This meant that the ingredients had gelled up. So Nelson took the glass pot over to the sink and told Kevin to get the ice. Nelson proceeded to turn the cold water on and let it run into the glass pot. Kevin splashed about five handfuls of ice into the pot. A minute later, Kevin turned the water off. I watched as the two of them acted as though they were cooking a full coarse meal. Nelson drained the water from the pot, and there along the bottom was a large thick cookie of street ready cocaine. Nelson took about six sheets of paper towels and laid them on the table. Then he dumped the cocaine cookie on the paper towels and asked me for a bath towel. I fetched the towel, then he took the large cocaine cookie and wrapped it up in the towel. Nelson patted the cookie for a minute, then unwrapped it and put it on the triple beam scale. It weighed 256 grams.

Kevin said, "Y'all do the math. There are nine ounces in a quarter kilo, and there are twenty eight grams in an ounce. Therefore, nine times twenty eight grams equal two hundred and fifty two grams. Look, the scale is showing 256 grams, which means it's still damp.

"We gave Nelson and Kevin fifteen hundred dollars for showing us how to cook the cocaine into crack. They also tried to sell us a recipe on how to stretch or blow up our crack for five grand. We told them that we were good, so we passed on that. They also asked us did we need a good connection, because they had it like Burger King and we can have it our way. Once again we told them that we were alright for now, because we had a good powder cocaine connection.

Since we were dealing crack now, we had to increase our security and hire workers. The crack rock turned the city into a complete mad house. People were now stealing like never before, killing and robbing. The prostitution business grew, but the pimps made less money because the prostitutes was selling their bodies for crack instead of cash. There were also black and white women that weren't previously prostituting, now they were hooked on crack and selling their bodies as well. They would trade anything for crack, including food stamps. Most of the women in the John Hayes Homes, Brandon Court, and Evergreen City allowed me and other crack dealers to set up shop in their homes in return for crack and financial support. I would have three or four guys selling the potent drug from the houses, and at least one of them would always have a gun. I didn't take into consideration that these women had young children. The only thing that I cared about was that all mighty dollar.

We supplied most of the lower level dealers with crack. We used pagers at that time to enhance our lines of communication with our crew as well as others. One day while I was chilling in the projects with my family, we decided to shoot dice. Even though we were family and one big posse, we still took the dice game serious in betting each other. After playing for about two hours, a couple of dealers walked up and asked us could they join in.

We all said, "sure, we don't mind." One of the guys came in the game on fire, making about five straight points, but he turned right around and missed on maybe the next seven. While waiting on my turn to shoot the dice, I looked down beside me and saw a wad of money on the ground. I reached down quickly and grabbed the money and put it in my pocket without counting it. As the dice came around to me, the guy that was standing beside me had something to say . . .

"Which one of you country niggas got my money?" Neither of us responded to him, we just kept on shooting dice. Then he spoke again, "One of you niggas better up my money right now before it be a problem!" Now, even though I was standing beside the guy, he accused my brother, Cheek of of having his money. Maybe that was because Cheek had came over closer to us. But the reason. that Cheek came over by us was to grab a beer which was sitting in the cooler behind us. I missed my point and the guy named Black stated pushing and shoving with Cheek. My brother, Joseph told Cheek to step back and let him whip Black. We immediately broke the fight up. Black and the other guy walked off promising that they would return. My brother, Joseph wasn't going to stand by and be punked out by nobody.

"Whatever niggas, I'll be right here," said Joseph." We went right on back to shooting dice. After they left we didn't even talk about the money, nor did anyone ask who had found the guy's money. At this time I wouldn't have admitted that I had the money anyway.

About forty five minutes later, Black and his crew came back. They really caught us slipping. All of them ran up on us with their guns out yelling-" break yourself niggas! Give it all up and we mean all of it!" As we were taking everything out of our pockets, Big Daddy, who was Cheeks guy, his gun got stuck around his waist, so one of the guys thought that he was trying to make a move on them. The guy from Black's crew slapped Big Daddy with his pistol in the jaw so hard that I felt it. After Black and his buddies picked up our money, guns, dope, and gold chains and watches, they said, "we don't want to see you niggas posted up out here selling dope anymore." They walked off hollering . . .

"Almighty! V.L.—Vice Lord's!"

Once Black and his guys left, we made sure that everybody was okay, especially Big Daddy. Then we told everyone that they did the right thing by giving up without a fight, because we understood that we could always get more dope, money, gold chains and watches, or whatever else, but we can't replace our lives. In other words, we told our workers as well as each other to never try to be a hero during a stick-up, because you may end up a zero by getting killed. Of course we also begin plotting on how we would retaliate in the next few days.

The next day, while sitting alone on the rail in the project with my lemon squeeze nine millimeter, one of the guys who robbed us, his sister came out of the radio station house. She looked over and saw me, so she walked over to me.

"What's up L.J., you must be waiting on your girl," she inquired?

"Nope. I'm just chillin. What's up with you, Patricia," I replied?

"Nothing much. I just called my brother and told him to come and get me."

"Hey Pat, your brother is ballin, huh?"

"Not like you country boys. Y'all got it going on for real." she said.

I never told Patricia that I had a beef with her brother. About fifteen minutes later, Patricia's brother was coming down the middle of the projects.

He was in his 1992 red Maxima, even though it was still 1991. He could see her because she was in the middle of the street, but I made my way between two cars. Once he stopped, right before Patricia could get in the passenger door, I had snatched his door open and put my nine millimeter to his head.

"Bitch ass nigga, you didn't think you was going to get away with it did you? Give me everything you got nigga," I demanded! "I'm not joking. Make my day." His name was Reggie and he didn't say a word. He just handed me his gun, his bank roll, his watch, and his gold charm, because he knew I was somewhat crazy from when we played on a youth basketball team together. While I was robbing Reggie, his sister was screaming for me not to kill her brother. As I back away from his car I said, "I should kill you nigga, but I like your mom and your sister." I went on and got into my car and drove away.

The next night we caught Reggie, Black, and some more of the their crew members slipping, coming out of a prostitute's house in the projects, after following one of the guys from Reggie's mom's house. As we ran up on them, they surrendered and asked for peace because they were also at war with the Metro Gang from St. Louis. they asked us to give them a list of everything that they took from us, so that they could square us away. Then they asked us to team up with them, but I told them that we were neutral and we wouldn't give them any assistance in a dispute with other gangs.

As the summer of 1992 came around, I decided to do my own thing, but continue to pool my money with the family to purchase large amounts of cocaine. My street image was growing day by day during this time. I was balling out of control and women were sweating me left and right, even though they knew I had a woman. I went and bought a 1992, white mini van with thin red stripes on both sides. I had a new Alpine sound system and I had an alarm installed on the same day. A couple of days later, I went and got both of the side windows and the back window tinted with limousine tint.

The next day around noon, I decided to go and show my ride off while checking my traps; in other words, checking my money. As I pulled up into the Fifteenth Street parking lot and got out of the car, all eyes were on me with several of my family members screaming, "Woo Daddy, Woo Daddy, boy you're looking like Nino Brown." After kicking the bo-bo for a while, we all threw fifty dollars in for a BBQ. A couple of my brothers girlfriends went to Shop N-Save to grab some meat, beer and other items. While the women was gone to the store, we had the neighborhood junk man to to go around to my sister Annie's house and grab our homemade fifty gallon barrel grill. Junk man charged me a twenty dollar rock for the job.

As the women got back from the store with the meat and other goods, I went into the house and seasoned the pork chops and ground beef for the hamburgers. I used Lowery's Seasoning and butter garlic on the pork chops.

As for the ground beef, I used lipton's onion mix and a little Lowery's Seasoning, then patted them into nice patties before wrapping them in foil.

A few of the women made some baked beans and spaghetti.

"Y'all don't think that we're going to eat this spaghetti do you," I joked?

"Why not," one of them asked me?

"y' all will never get us like that," I said while laughing! "We're real familiar with the spaghetti trick." They all laughed.

"Don't give us no ideas, plus it's not that time of them month for me," they all said at the same time.

As I came out of the house with the large pans of meat, everybody was asking, "Woo Daddy, what do you have in the aluminum foil?"

"Woo Daddy's famous burgers," I replied. Joseph and Me were doing our thing on the grill while my nephew Alfred went out to his low-rider truck and turned his concert sound system on blast. The next thing I knew, the yard was full of people . . . and we fed them all. They were dancing and drinking as if they were at a free party. There were these two crackheads at the BBQ named Tommy-T and Spiderman. I asked them if they would help me clean up when we were done. They both said, yes, but also told me that they needed a hit; meaning some crack rock to get the monkey off their back. I called one of my workers over and had him to give them both a a crack rock. Those two jokers took off like a jet.

There was this pretty chocolate sexy lady that kept walking by the cookout, but she never stopped. I could tell that she was what we called fresh meat. Once the cookout ended, Spiderman and Tommy-T took care of their clean up duties for me. My nephew Alfred threw both of them a twinkie bag of crack.

A few days later, I gave Tommy-T a job selling crack for me. I didn't mind hiring a smoker, because I knew what to expect from them. I knew that once they got their medicine, they was going to take care of business for me.

Truthfully, the three smokers I had working for me was the best husters on my team. Now, on the other hand, it was always the closet smokers that hid their habit that I had to worry about. They would run down a hundred excuses why my money was messed up. They would tell stories like; I got robbed, or a crackhead ran off with the money, or the lie that topped them all was that they had to throw the dope because the po-po ran up on them. Then come to find out, they were getting high off my dope and trying to front like they had it going on.

Now, since I was now on my won, I decided that it was time for me to go into the cooking lab so I could keep folks out of my business. So I went out to Penny Lane and bought me my own triple beam scale. Then I went to Big Lot and grabbed a large glass pot, oven mits, sandwich bags, and a large plastic cake mixing bowl. Then I drove out to my stash house on fourteenth Street and South Grand. I decided to pass by the house just in case someone was following me, then I went back to my stash house. I entered the house with my bag of paraphernalia and immediately locked the door. I grabbed a quarter kilo of powder cocaine, then I dumped the drugs into the cake bowl. I then weighed out six ounces of baking soda and mixed it with the cocaine. I filled the glass pot about half full with water and put it on the stove and allowed it to boil. Once the water started boiling, I added the dope and baking soda, then turned the stove off. I then shook the glass pot for about two or three minutes hoping and praying that I didn't screw up. A few minutes later, it began to gel up and I smile in relief. I rushed the glass pot over to the sink and let the cold water run slowly into the pot while I grabbed the ice.

Shortly after I put the ice into the pot, it turned into a hard, thick cookie of crack cocaine. I told myself, "I'm Chef Woo Daddy and I'm the real deal."

After I dumped the crack cookie onto the towel and dabbed it dry, then I put it onto the scale. It weighed 258 grams. I did the math to ensure that I was truly Chef Woo Daddy. I replayed the measurements in my head, "Nine times twenty eight grams equal 252 grams, but I got two hundred and fifty eight grams. Dang, I'm good." The extra six grams was because the dope was still wet.

I was twenty eight years old and flamboyant. I felt like I was on top of the world, in fact I was in my own world . . . L.J.'s Crack World! People were really stroking my image or shall I say my ego at this time. They were telling me, "Woo Daddy, you got the best damn crack in town. You're the man with the plan, and the doctor with the medicine that I need." I must keep it real with you though, this is the time that the image man that other people as well as myself had created became grown. Nobody could tell me anything, not even God.

I was foolish out of my mind. I never gave it any thought that I was destroying so many people's lives. Most of all, it never crossed my mind that I was part of a conspiracy to bring crack babies into the world. I never seen the big picture, all I saw was dollar signs-$$$. There were warning signs flashing before my eyes and my conscience would speak to me and people confirm what my conscience was saying to me. They would tell me, "Son, L.J., your name is ringing, you need to slow down or better yet, quit!" I never really took heed to the warning signs. Now I know that it was God trying to get my attention.

I decided to take a trip to Mississippi to see my mother and to take a break from all of the madness that was going on in my crack world. I left the drug business to my guy, Donut until I got back. While on my way to my mother's house I had a talk with myself. "I do need to slow down. This way I can spend more time with my children," I told myself. Once I got to Memphis I stopped at the mall and grabbed a couple of outfits just in case I decided to stay longer at my mom's house. Then I headed on down the highway on the way to mom's house. When I arrived at my mother's house, I felt a great sense of peace that had come over me. After sitting in my ride for about forty five minutes, thinking, I got out of my car and walked into mom's house. She was so excited to see me, but I could tell that she knew that something was bothering me. I couldn't believe that she didn't question me. A couple of minutes later, my stepfather came into the living room. We talked for a while, and afterward I gave my mother four hundred dollars and a sixty five dollar book of food stamps, and whatever else she needed. I looked at the clock and it said noon. It had only taken me about seven and a half hours to make the trip from Illinois to Mississippi. I asked my mom to wake me up by six p.m.

I turned my pager off and fell into a dead sleep.

Around 5:45 p.m. my mother came into the bedroom and woke me up, but I didn't get up. I guess I was just so tired that I couldn't, and my body was letting know it. One thing about the human body that I have experienced, over a period of time, if you don't shut it down, it will shut down on its own.

So I finally got up around 9:00 p.m. Before I could ask my mother why she didn't wake me up at six o'clock, she said, "son I could tell that you was tired from the minute that you walked through the door, not just from the drive here."

Since it was Friday night, I decided to take a shower and go out on the town. I threw on my Chicago Bulls jean outfit and my red and black Jordan's, and my fitted white bulls cap. Then I hit the door and headed to the Cotton Club. As I entered the Club, all eyes were on me. The club was packed and full with fine chicks. I went over to the bar and got me a coke and a glass of ice and then found me a table. Once I stopped at the table three nice young ladies in their early twenties came over to me.

"Excuse us, they said. "This is our table. We just went to dance. "No problem ladies," I replied. "I didn t know that someone was sitting here, I'll leave."

"You don't have to leave J with your fine ass one of them said. "We're here alone. It's our girl, Brenda's birthday." After they introduced themselves to me, I bought them a bottle of champagne, a couple forty ounces of Old English, and a pint of Gin in hopes that it would make them sin, if you know what I mean. I also ordered a couple of cans of orange juice and coke. After kicking it with Brenda, Peaches, and Linda for a while I told each of them their last names. They asked me how in the world did I know their last names.

"Ms. Cleo is my aunt," I said. "I'm psychic."

"Yea right," said Brenda. "Somebody told you who we were."

"You trippin, that can't be true. You guys wasn't at the table when I walked in," I said. Before they could respond, I asked Brenda, "how about a slow dance from the birthday lady?"

"Sure," she said! "This is my favorite song—If This World Were Mine. This song just do something to me."

While dancing with Brenda I asked her, "are you still with Willie Joe?"

"Hell no, he ran off to Springfield, Illinois with a fat bitch named Jalina." Brenda and I also danced the next song, because she was questioning me, trying to figure out how I knew so much about her and she knew nothing about me other than my name was Woo Daddy, and that I was from Illinois.

As we got back to the table, Peaches and Linda said to Brenda, "Dang we thought y'all fell in love on the dance floor."

"I know you bitches ain't hating on me on my birthday," said Brenda.

"Check this out bitch," they continued to joke around. "We know what's up with you, you're trying to get some Chicago dick tonight."

"You got that right, bitches," said Brenda.

"You young ladies are wild," I said.

As a quarter til two rolled around, the bartender yelled last call for alcohol, I didn't mind treating the ladies since I had plenty of money. I asked Brenda, Linda, and Peaches would they like another drink before they go. All three of them agreed on Gin and Juice. I then asked Brenda, "since this is the last song for the night, let me have another slow dance. The D.J. played: "Close The Door" by T.P., a.k.a.

The one and only Teddy Pendgrass.

While Brenda and I was slow dancing, Peaches and Linda came up to us and said, "I knew he was somebody that we knew. Brenda, this is Lynwood that played basketball for Cleveland High. He lived across the railroad tracks on Daisy Road."

"I know you're not the Lynwood that I think you are," said Brenda? I don't know why I didn't catch on to your unique voice." At this point I could no longer keep a straight face.

"Now what?" That was all I could say.

"We're gong to spend the night with you at your hotel room."

We left the Cotton Club and went and rented a room with double beds at the Holiday Inn. About fifteen minutes after we got in the room, Peaches and Linda passed out. Brenda and I got in my ride and went to the gas station.

We grabbed some nachos with cheese, and a box of Trojans. When we got back to the room, Peaches and Linda were still knocked out. Once we finished eating, Brenda and I got busy. She was a real freak in bed. As she removed her clothes, I couldn't believe how well built she was. There wasn't a single mark on her body. She kissed me on every part of my body . . . yea even there, and the blow job was out of this world. She acted as though it was just the two of us in the room. The whole time we were getting busy, she was talking dirty to me and asking me questions. Believe it or not, Peaches and Linda didn't even move. We took a shower together around five a.m., then we took a fast detour to the bed and fell asleep.

We all woke up around the same time. I got up and got myself together.

Once we left, I dropped them off at Brenda's mother's house. As I got to my mother's house around noon, she had cooked me my favorite meal; Fried chicken, greens, cornbread, stewed sweet potatoes, sock it to me cake, and there was a six pack of Nehi Peach soda in the refrigerator.

After spending a couple more days with my mother and visiting my grandmother, I headed back to Springfield. On my way back home, I heard a voice saying, "son, what you're doing is not what I have planned for you."

I guess that was God speaking to me that time. Now at this time, I was too deep in the game. Too many people were depending on me, and plus I had gone too far to turn around, at least I thought. In all actuality, I was just caught up in the game and the cares of the world. I can honestly say that the trip to Mississippi gave me a sense of peace that I hadn't had in a long time. I didn't have to keep looking over my shoulder for the police or the stick-up boys, and all of the drama that came along with being a high rolling drug dealer. I felt as free as a bird and I had no worries.

CHAPTER 7

A COLD CRACK WORLD

Once I got back to the crib, I went straight to the project to find Donut, and check my traps. In spite of myself talk and the voice that I perceived to be God that I heard on my way home, I found myself trapped right back in my crack world again. As I got to the project, I seen my brother, Head and a couple of his workers posted up. I went and parked my van and went over and kicked it with them for a minute. After a few minutes Head told me that he wanted to holler at me for a second.

"Your guy Donut and your nephew, Loco got into a shoot-out with each other," said Head. "Woo Daddy, they was trippin. The bad thing about it, they shot this crack-head named Harry. I'm surprised that they only shot him."

"Did he die," I asked?

"Nope, but he lost one of his eyes. Donut was the one who shot him. Oh yea, Woo Daddy, we gave him a quarter kilo so he wouldn't press charges on Donut. We also gave out a bunch of bags, cause the whole project seen it.," Head said.

"I'll swing by Harry mom's house to see what's up," I said. After talking to Head, I paged Donut. I entered J-911-2, which was our code for hit me back A.S.A.P. A couple of minutes later my pager went off. It was Donut.

I hurried and called back the number that he left in my pager.

"What's up—fool. Where you at? I'm back" I said.

"That's good I'm at my cousin James house in Brandon Court. We need to talk," said Donut.

My reply was, "I'll be there in ten minutes."

I jumped in my van and headed over to Brandon Court to scoop up Donut.

As soon as I pulled up, he came out and got into the van.

"Hey fool," I said. "I know you don't have no heat on you or no work?"

"Woo Daddy stop playing. I know your rules." We rode out to Motel Six so that we could talk. Once we got inside the room, Donut began telling me what happened between he and Loco. He told me that Loco had tried to beat him out of an eight ball of crack, so he confronted Loco about it. That's when lie says Loco fronted on him and called him a bitch ass nigga.

"Donut, you should've hit that nigga right there, dead in his mouth," I said!

"Man, I didn't want to fight him around your family."

"Donut, check this out . . . let one of your family members try that junk with me. I bet we are going to get busy right there," I replied.

So he rattled on telling me the rest. "So I went to my car and got my heat, and as I was coming back across the street, Loco went to busting at me. So I busted back at the fool. The punk took off running after he shot at me a couple more times, so I chased him and shot at him a few more times," said Donut.

"Bu t you didn't hit him?"

"Nope, but I shot this crackhead named Harry."

"Now how in the hell did you shoot the crackhead and you was shooting at Loco?" I just laughed.

"Loco had ran over by a tree and as the crackhead peeped around the tree the bullet hit him in the eye. Shoot, then I ran back to my car and left."

"Where is your car now," I asked?

"It's in the back of Carissa's house in Evergreen City," he answered.

"So how did business go while I was gone?"

"Everything is gone except for the packs that we have on the street," he replied.

"Damn I should have re'd-up before I left. I didn't think you would have scored eighty six before I got back," I said. Eighty six means sold out in dope man terms.

"Woo Daddy, all of the money is in the safe and everything is accounted for. We have about five grand on the streets."

"That's cool homie. You just might be ready to go solo, but we better go and see what's up with this shooting issue. I'm going to go by the county building and speak to this cop that I know," I said.

After getting back from the county building, I gave Donut the 4-1-1.

There was now a warrant out for Donut's arrest. We couldn't figure out who turned him in. The officer only told me that a young lady called, but she didn't give her name.

Nevertheless, I told Donut, "you need to go and turn yourself in, because we will be taking a serious risk trying to get money with a warrant hanging over your head. The minute that they give you a bond, I'll be there to get you out."

"Woo Daddy, I know that. Hey, I need you to go and get De De for me, and an ounce of skunk bud."

"Man,—you're a weedhead, but you're good for that," I replied. I wasted no time in taking care of Donut's request. About forty five minutes later, I returned with De De, the ounce of skunk bud, and a forty ounce of Old English. Then I told Donut that I'd be back in a couple of hours.

I headed over to the crib to let Robbin know that I was back. As I walked through the door, she went off on me.

"Why in the hell didn't you call me?!"

"Who in the hell do you think you are talking to me like that," I asked?

"I'm talking to you punk," she replied! After looking at Robbin for about a minute, I spoke again.

"Bitch, you must have fell and bumped your head while I was gone."

"Fuck you, punk! I'll solve this problem right now . . . get your shit and get out of my house!"

"I don't have a problem with it. As a matter of fact, you're doing me a favor," I said. I had already moved my clothes out before I went to Mississippi. As I was walking out of the door, I stopped and told her, "do me a favor and let my name taste like shit in your mouth."

I got into my car and headed to the hotel to get Donut. Once I got there, I paged Donut to let him know that I was back. About five minutes later, he and De De came out and got into the van. On our way to the county building, we stopped by KFC and pigged out. After eating, we made our way to the county building. Before going inside, Donut gave me his pager and a wad of money. We got out and walked inside. I gave him a hug and told his to stay focussed and not to worry. I let him know that I was getting him a lawyer and he would get him a bond."

On my way out of the building, I stopped by the control desk and put three hundred dollars on his books so that he could by commissary.

After I drpped De De off at her crib, I went to my stash house to count my money that Donut had made while I was out of town. Just he had said, everything was accounted for, except the five thousand that was in the street. I hit Cheek up on his pager and entered J-86-911 in it.

About ten minutes later Cheek hit me back and told me to come out to his girl Tanya's house on Knot Street. As I got to Cheek's house, we made plans to get a mother's load.

A few days later I was back in business. While sitting in Evergreen City, Reggie and a couple of his guys rode up on me.

"What's up Coach? I still got those cheap bricks," said Reggie.

"I'm good, but I will keep that in mind," I replied. It turned out to be a blessing that I decided not to deal with Reggie, because a month after our conversation the Feds snatched him and his posse up on a drug conspiracy charge. When Reggie's trial started my name came up all throughout the trial.

Kevin, who was one of the guys that taught me how to cook cocaine into crack, became an informant for the government. He testified at Reggie's trial. A young lady told me that while Reggie was on the witness stand he said that I was one of Reggie's workers and he had helped me count over ten thousand dollars before to give to Reggie. She told me that Reggie's attorney asked "is Mr. Joiner being charged in this case?" The attorney for the government told him no, that Mr. Joiner is not being charged. Since they said that I wasn't being charged, I took it to be a license to continue, but keep it on the down low and I would be okay.

The next day I went to the projects to check my traps, I was told that my guys had met some girls from East St. Louis and was hanging out at their crib. I d.rove down to their apartment on 14th Place. As I pulled into the alley by the apartment, I blew my horn and a nice dark chocolate young lady came to the door. She had a very sexy voice. I could only see her face.

"Is Zang and Fo Fa there," I asked? A few seconds later Zang came out of the house. Once he got into the car, we turned a few corners as we talked.

"What's up man, I have been trying to call you for about a week. I hit Donut a couple of times and he didn't hit me back either, so we found some cuttie pies and we've been hanging out with them," said Zang. At that point I told Zang about Donut's situation. I couldn't believe it, but he hadn't heard about the shooting until I told him. Then I told him that his sister and I broke up.

"Woo Daddy, I love my sister, but I don't know how you put up with her shit for so long."

"One reason why is because I love your niece and nephew, and your family as a whole," I replied. Without hesitation Zang told me that he had a female for me. "I'm cool right now, I need to be free for a while," I answered.

"Let me know if you change your mind, and you just might do that when you see her. She's about 5' 7" and weigh about one hundred and thirty pounds, and she's very cool." After Zang and I finished talking, I dropped him back off at the crib. Before getting out of the van, he gave me five grand and told me that he needed some work bad. I told him that I'd hook him up in a couple of hours.

After being in jail for about two weeks, the judge gave Donut a fifteen thousand dollar bond, but he only had to pay ten percent of it. As soon as his cousin Carissa told me, I immediately went and bailed him out. I didn't do it personally though, just to keep my name out of the police files.

It was now November of 1992 and I had decided to take Zang up on his offer about hooking me up with the young lady. Okay now, guess who she was?

She was the same young lady that walking by the BBQ that we had in my nephew Alfred's backyard. Zang invited me to go in the house with him. When we got inside, he introduced me to everyone. The young lady's mom spoke up.

"Which one of my daughters do you like," she asked? I just smiled because I hadn't even met her daughter yet.

"He likes your youngest daughter, Evelyn," said Zang.

As Evelyn came down the stairs and saw me, she immediately went back up the stairs, but her mother called her.

"Evelyn, would you like to introduce your boyfriend to me?"

"I don't even know this boy," she replied. "I mean this man. Zang and Lisa hooked this up." I decided to speak up then.

"Zang just wanted me to meet his girl Lisa, and the family, and he asked me would I like to meet Evelyn." Ms. Jane was very respectful and friendly to me and my guys. Later that night I hooked up with Evelyn and she told me that she was in a relationship with her baby's dad, but she was trying to break up with him. About three days later, while sitting on the sofa with Evelyn, her child's father came over. As Evelyn introduced us I said . . . "what's up GMan?"

"What's up L.J.," he said. Then he asked Evelyn could he speak with her.

She excused herself so that they could talk privately. About fifteen minutes later she came back and told me that G-Man wanted to holler at me. I got up and went into the kitchen where he was.

"L. J. I don't know what Evelyn told you, but she's my woman. She's just been trippin with me."

"Check this out, G-Man I didn't know that this was your girl, but she told me that she was trying to break up with you, but that you keep sweating her. You know me and I'm not one to trip over a woman, because they come a dime a dozen."

"I'm 'not is woman, I'm just his baby mama," said Evelyn as she entered the kitchen.

"Evelyn, I don't want to cause any problems, so I'm going to leave," I said.

Her reply was, "you I re not going anywhere, he's going to leave." So I went back and took a seat on the couch. A few minutes later I heard Evelyn yelling at G-Man.

Get your hands off of me! I'm not gong anywhere with you!" Two of my buddies got up and went into the kitchen area. I thought they were going outside, but instead they threw G-Man outside. She told Ed and Fo *Fa* that she was okay. After G-Man left I put on my triple fat goose L.A. Kings coat and told Ed and Fo Fo to step outside with me for a minute. Once we were outside, I told them that they was wrong for getting in Evelyn and G-Man's business.

"You're right Woo Daddy, but that chump always comes over here trippin With her.

"Yea but still, that's not y'alls business, that's her business. I'm sure that she knows what to do when she get fed up with him for real," I said.

Once we got back inside the house, she tried to apologize to me, but I told her that there was no need to apologize, because she can't control GMan's actions or his feelings for her.

1993 rolled in and Evelyn was now pregnant after just being involved with me for four months. One day while chilling with Evelyn at her sister's house, a young lady knocked on the door and asked for me. I told Evelyn's sister, Lisa to tell the person at the door that she could find whatever she needed out on the corner. I thought that it was a crackhead. About five minutes later she came back to the door and asked for me again. I told Lisa to tell her to stop sweating me, and I will be out in a few minutes. Once again the young lady came back to the door. As Lisa opened the door, the young lady delivered a shocking message.

"Could you tell Woo Daddy that Carissa is pregnant with his child." I must say that Evelyn acted very mature about the situation.

"L.J.," said Evelyn. "You should go and talk to her and please come back and let me know what's up." Just as I got ready to go and talk to Carissa, Lisa asked me a question.

"Is that your yellow buick down there in the parking lot with the tinted windows," asked Lisa?

"Yep. That's mine."

"Well some girl is down there breaking your windows out," said Lisa. I ran out of the house and on down the street to the parking lot to see who it was. Of course it was Carissa. I ran up to her and took the stick from her.

"Are you losing your mind," I asked? She grabbed a bottle and busted against my car. I grabbed her and pushed her, then I told her brother, who was standing close by to come and get her before I break all two hundred and six bones in her body. I hopped in my my car and left so that I could cool off. I mumbled to myself how lucky she was that she didn't break my windows out, or I would've broke her tail.

After I cooled off, I went back to Lisa's house to get Evelyn. Then I took Evelyn out to eat so that we could talk.

"Evelyn I'm sorry about what happend at Lisa's house," I said. "Before I met you, I was messing around with her on the side. I promise you that I'm not messing with her now."

"Okay, all I ask you to do is to be straight up with me and respect me," she replied.

"You got that Sweetheart," I said. After eating, we drove to Evelyn's house. That's when she informed me that she was thinking about moving, so we went to get a newspaper so that we could look at the housing market and find a location. About three days later, we went and found us a nice two bedroom apartment. Without telling Evelyn, I went and bought us some brand new maroon furniture, and glass tables.

In the meantime the Feds grabbed Donut on a gun charge, because of the incident when he shot Crackhead Harry. The state had dropped the case against him. Since the Feds grabbed Donut, I became as nervous as a hooker in a church house, because I knew the feds was going to question him about me, but what I didn't know was how much pressure Donut could stand. You know the old saying "Pressure bust pipes." I became even more nervous when I didn't hear from Donut in over a week. So one day I went by De De's house. She' came to the door.

"You must knew that I needed to talk with you," she said.

"Not really, but I need to talk to you. Have you heard from Donut?"

"Yes, I sure have, and he told me to tell you that those people asked about you and your family. He also told me to tell you that the county building is packed with nigga's from the joint for some reason and you don't have to worry about him turning on you. Just look out for his son by Lavette."

"Okay," I said. Then I told De De to go and visit him on Sunday and put some money on his books for me.

"Sure I'll do that for you," she said. "I was planning to go and see him anyway.

"De De if you need anything, give me a page at this number 467-7136. De De make sure that you put your address in the page." That Sunday I took De De to visit Donut. We went by Popeye's Chicken to grab a bite to eat. While eating De De and I talked about Donut and her conversation concerning the Feds questioning about me.

"L.J. he said that the Feds is there every day questioning somebody about you and your family. He said that some guy there named Stutter-Man told him that he would be a damn fool not to tell on you and your family. He also told me to tell you that some girl is suppose to get you and set you and your family up for the Feds."

"Damn! The Feds are really on my tail. I'm going to chill for a couple of months."

"L. J. you should at least chill for a couple of months and see what's up with Donut."

"Thanks De De, that's what I'm going to do." About two months later, a guy that I know by the name of Speck stopped me in the John Hay Homes.

"Woo Daddy," said Speck. "I think your guy Donut gave you and your family up to the Feds. I overheard him and Dirty Blue talking about those

people were trying to get them to go to the grand jury on you and your family."
It seemed that every time dudes was being released from the county jail,
they would find me and tell me that the Feds are questioning people about
us. Most of them were smokers, so it would go in one ear and out the other.
There were times that it would cross my mind, but the fear only lasted for
short period of times.

After being out of town for about three weeks, I decided to go to the John
Hayes Homes to check on the family. When I got there and walked up to
the crib where the family was hanging out at, I saw a young lady who I knew
was suppose to be in federal prison! Nevertheless, I blew it off and gave the
family dap. I didn't speak to the female, nor did she say anything to me. Then
I thought about what De De had told me that Donut had told her that a girl
is suppose to be getting out of the joint to set me and my family up for the
Feds. Strangely, it was August and the girl had on shorts with a jacket, and on
one leg was an electric leg monitor. I looked her up and down, then I called
Cheek and Monika over. Then we walked on into the house.

"Are y' all crazy," I asked? "That girl is suppose to be in federal prison.
She got a leg monitor on her leg. She could be wired up." Cheek didn't feel
my vibe.

"Woo Daddy, slow down, you're trippin. She's over here with Monika. You
know Alice, she's cool," Cheek insisted.

"I'm sorry bro, but it don't set well with me. I'm out of here," I said.

"L.J., she is not the police if that's what you're thinking," Monika said.
Looking back, I realize that I should have told Cheek and Monika what Donut
had said, but I figured that they wouldn't believe it, because he was in jail.
At that point I left.

A couple of weeks later, I went to the store to get some milk and on my
way back to the house, I noticed a blue Chevy was following me. As I got out
of my car in my driveway, the clean cut white man yelled . . .

"Mr. Joiner, how's your crack world going?" I threw my hands up in the
air in a daring manner. Then he said, "I will see you around soon."

It was now December of 1993 and Carissa and Evelyn both had their
baby within a month apart from each other. They both had boys: Yada and
Zo. As Christmas came around and I had the Christmas spirit. I invited both
my family and Evelyn's family over for a special dinner. I made chicken
& dressing, glazed ham with cherry's and pineapples, BBQ chicken, ribs,
collard greens with ham hocks, mac and cheese, potato salad, sweet potato
pies, and three cakes: lemon, chocolate, and caramel. I made sure that I had
chiterlings with plenty of hot sauce, cranberry sauce, soda, beer, wine, and
gin. Both sides of the family was very impressed with the meal.

Something I must point out about the Feds is that they will turn family against family and let you know who's your true friends. I entered 1994 knowing that the Feds was on my tail, and it had began to rest heavily on my mind that maybe Donut had gave me up to the Feds and cut my throat along with several other cut-throat individuals. I was now about to learn that the crack world was extremely cold and full of cut—throats,

CHAPTER 8

L.J.'s HABIT OR ADDICTION

Although I was known to be a square from Delaware; meaning that I didn't smoke cigarettes, didn t drink, or didn't get high in any shape form or fashion with any drugs, I had a habit or addiction that I believe is worse than any of the three . . . gambling. Every day while hanging out hustling, I would shoot dice or play cards. It would be me, Bankhead, Keith, and this nickel slick joker named Memphis. One day while playing cards I won about twenty five hundred dollars, so they wanted to switch the game to dice.

"Cool. You niggas are the losers, so make it easy on yourselves." Memphis passed me a new set of red dice. I threw seven and eleven back to back as if I had license to gamble. Whenever I caught a point, I would throw it right back in the door. After shooting dice for about ten minutes, one of my best customers walked up to me and told me that he needed to speak to me for a minute and that it was important. When we got around the corner, Ted gave me fifty crisp one hundred dollar bills. I told him to page me in a couple of hours. Then I took the money that he gave me and put in my trunk safe. Once I returned to the dice game, Memphis was shooting the dice.

"Woo Daddy, do you still think you're hot," asked Memphis? I didn't even think before I replied.

"Give me the dice, I can show you better than I can tell you." Memphis began to catch my dice after I made about five straight licks. As he caught the dice, he shook them in his hand and blew on them. After Memphis caught the dice I never made another point nor did I throw another seven or eleven on the first roll. Now, since I couldn't throw a lick, I began to side bet with Keith who was passing. All of a sudden he threw more snake eyes that I'd ever seen before, after Bankhead had caught the dice. It didn't take long for., me to lose the five grand that I had won, plus five hundred of my own money.

After the game was over, Keith and I couldn't believe how our luck had taken such a drastic turn for the worse. That's when Keith told me that he was pretty sure that Bankhead and Memphis had slid some trick dice in the game.

I was totally green or naive when it came to recognizing loaded or trick dice.

Keith told me how people slip trick dice into the game. He said they would have a pair of trick dice in their hand, so that when they catch the dice and shake them in their hand, they would put the trick dice down and pretend that they ate putting money in their pocket. What also went into their pocket though was the good dice.

"Keith, I know you didn't let those nigga' s get us," I said.

"Woo Daddy, you know me better than that. If I ever catch those suckers doing it, I would take their life on the spot and I mean that on my mother's grave."

There were night when I would go on the gambling boat and wouldn't tell nobody. I would play blackjack all night long. I would win several thousand dollars, then sit there and lose it all back like darn fool. Most of the time I would even lose a couple thousand of my own money. On my way back to the crib I would talk to myself. "I got to stop this gambling crap and get back focussed on my hustling game. I'm hustling backwards," I would tell myself.

My gambling habit or addiction had began to take a toll on my relationship. Evelyn started to complain about me staying out every night.

One time I came home around three a.m. and Evelyn was sitting up watching television. As soon as I walked through the door, she started yapping.

"L. J., we need to talk right now."

"Okay, give me about five minutes and we can talk," I replied. Once I took care of my bankroll, I came back into the living room and talked with Evelyn. Her first question was a long way from gambling.

"Are you seeing somebody else," she asked? "If you are let me know. I found a phone number in your pocket with a woman's name on it." She showed me the number, and it was the a number to the Springfield Housing Authority with Nancy on it. Nancy was the clerk at the front desk. I told Evelyn that she could call the number, but I had a better idea . . . I grabbed the phone and called the number. I turned the speaker phone on so that she could hear it.

"Well you still need to get your priorities in order and start coming home at a decent hour," she said. "You need to spend some time with me and the kids."

"Pump your breaks woman, you knew what I was doing when you met me. I'm not going to let you stop me from doing my thing."

"If you don't get your shit together, I'm going to leave you," she threatened.

"Do whatever you feel is best for you. I can't be in two places at one time, so if you don't like what I'm doing, be my guest and hit the road."

"You must think I'm with you for your money, "I got my own Money."

"That's good, so let me get mine.

"You need to be careful or better yet, you should get you a real damn job," she said.

"Evelyn, I know what I'm doing. Once I get enough money so that we can live comfortable, I'm going to quit."

"Okay L.J., you know what you're doing. Just keep on doing you, and remember that I told you so."

"Come on now girl, you know that I'm a good man and I just want to provide for you and the children," I said.

"You're a good provider, but you're not a good family man. We need your time way more than your money or anything else." I would break down and do the right thing for about a week, then I would go right back to being my old self. I must keep it real with you, I didn't think that I had a habit or addiction. To me, gambling was a part of being a drug dealer or hustler, just something that went along with the show-boating lifestyle.

My gambling problem slowly began to creep into my crack business and confused my priorities. There were times that my pager would be blowing up, but I wouldn't answer it because I was gambling. There were also times when I I would be a day late on picking up the package from my connection, because I was gambling. As time passed, my gambling habit or addiction got so bad that I could barely stay above water. In other words I was struggling to live the dope man lifestyle. The only thing that helped me was Evelyn. She was not a gold digger, and Cheek had my back along with Head. I decided to get my life back on track. I took a job with the Housing Authority after Shay left me a message with Evelyn. They hired me as a Youth Specialist Supervisor at the Johnson Park Community Center.

Now that I had a job again, I felt safer selling crack on the down-low.

A month after being hired, I was given a drug test. I certainly was not worried about failing the drug test since I was a drug free square from Delaware.

One morning on my way to work, I stopped by Carissa's house and had sex with her. When I was finished I took a shower so that I wouldn't smell like sardines at work. I took a good look at my son Yada who was asleep, then I left.

I got back in my car and headed on to work. As I drove along, I noticed the same blue Chevy that I had seen in 1993 following me again. When I pulled up to the Community Center and got out of my car, the guy that was driving the blue Chevy had something smart to say . . .

"So we meet again huh, Mr. Joiner. It's good to know that you have a job. I'll see you soon." I didn't even bother to respond, I just walked into the Community Center. I went into my office and took a deep breath saying, "damn" to myself. They were really on my trail. I couldn't believe it, but Donut must have given me up. My entire day at work was messed up. All types of things ran through my head. Now I believed that theory about four thousand thoughts running through a person's mind a day.

On my way home after work, I was nervous as all out doors and constantly looking in my rear view mirror. Once I got to the crib, I stayed inside.

Evelyn kept asking me what was wrong with me. I told her that I had a long hard day at work. She asked me what I would like to eat. So I asked her the same question.

"What would you like to eat," I asked her?

"Baby, I would love to have some of your fried spaghetti with meat sauce and some catfish nuggets," she replied. I immediately got up and prepared Evelyn and the kids the meal that she had requested. After having dinner, we watched a few movies before going to bed.

About three weeks later while I was at work, I got a call from the main office. It was my supervisor's secretary on the phone. She informed me that my supervisor, Mr. Moore wanted to see me right away in his office.

"Could you please tell him that we're serving lunch right now," I replied.

She put me on hold, then told me, "Mr. Moore said you must come over now." Once I hung the phone up I called my assistant, Kate into the office and told her to handle things for a few minutes. I told her that they needed me over at the main office right away. Kate asked me what was wrong. She wondered if it was a family issue and she offered her help if I needed it.

"I don't know what it is, Kate, I'll see when I get there."

I got into my cat and headed over to the main office. Once I got there and walked through the door, all eyes was on me. I strolled over to me friend's desk and asked her, "Lynn, what's up? What's going on?"

"L.J., all I know is that there are rumors floating around that you failed the drug test." Now that got a laugh out of me.

"Stop playing. You know I don't driuk, smoke, or nothing," I replied.

A couple of minutes later, my supervisor's cut little secretary came out and told me that Mr. Moore was ready to see me. I walked into Mr. Moore's office and he told me to have a seat.

"You're doing a wonderful job at the Center," he said.

"Thank you sir," I said.

"Remember that drug test that we had you take a while back, it came back positive."

"Sir, you must be joking," I said.

"I wish I was joking, because you're a damn good worker."

"Yea but Mr. Moore, this must be a mistake, because I don't drink, smoke, or do drugs," I pleaded.

"Lynard, I had them to check it again to make sure there was not a mix up, because I know you don't do drugs and I certainly don't get that perception from you."

"Do you want me to go and take the test over, sir.?"

"That won't be necessary Lynard, according to our policy, I must terminate you immediately. I need you to turn your keys in and you can come and pick up your check on the fifteenth. Now go and clean yourself up and we will think about hiring you back." I threw my keys on his desk. I wanted to tell him to tell his mama to clean herself up, but I didn't. I just walked out the office and slammed the door behind me.

I'm sure you're wondering how I failed the drug test when I had never used drugs. The answer is easy. While cooking the crack cocaine I didn't wear a mask or gloves. Therefore the drugs got into my system through my pores.

Now that I lost my job, I became even more suspicious of Alice being around the family. To top it off, she was now going with Monika to pick up the drugs for us. About three days after I lost my job, I went over to the family's hang out spot, and guess who was there . . . yeap, it was Alice. Once again I called Cheek saying, "y'all got more guts than I got, I could never be comfortable with her around me."

"Bro, check this out," said Cheek. "I really don't deal with her or talk to her about drugs. She's only seen me smoking weed."

"That's good, but watch her. Something's just not right about this picture, I'm telling you. And oh yea, you be sure to tell Monika not to ever bring Alice to my house with her," I told him. I guess Cheek delivered my message to Monika, because I noticed a change in our relationship. I finally figured out why the O' Jays came out with their song, "Money." That mean green almighty dollar will separate family, love ones, and the best of friends. I'm not saying that money is a bad thing, because we need money to purchase life necessities. The Bible say—"For the love of money is the root of all evil."

My reason for saying that about the almighty green dollar and the love of money will separate family, love ones, and friends, well one day my nephew D.C. and my cousin Jason and one of his friends got into a fight about some drug money that came up short. The fight between me and them turned into a small family fued, but because of the family closeness resolved our dispute quickly.

As drug dealers, most of us became images of the streets. We were blind, closed minded, hard headed, and self seeking. Therefore, we didn't want to hear anything about our lifestyles and what we were doing. We didn't take the sound advice from people telling us things for our own good. We would justify our actions by saying that we was trying to feed our families, so we had to do what we had to do. Our favorite two sayings when people told us that out name was ringing in the streets and that we need to slow down was, "I ain't doing nothing or they're just hating on me."

One day I went to the County Building to visit Carissa's brother who had caught an attempted murder case. His name was Thin-Man.

"L.J., this dude named Black Joe told me to tell you that the Feds is coming to get you and your family, but they said that they really don't want you. They said they must get you to make things right."

"Yea, you tell him that I'm not doing nothing, but I know their cut throat asses are back to tell on me and my family, but I'm good."

Several weeks later, the Feds snatched Monika and her posse. We knew at that point that it wouldn't be long before they came to get us. About six months after the Feds locked up Monika, she called to the family's house crying. She asked to speak to Cheek. He put her on speaker phone so that we all could hear.

"Cheek, these people want you, and they want me to tell on you. They told me that if I don't do it, I will never see my kids again." Cheek didn't even hesitate before making his remark.

"Do whatever you got to do, better me than you," said Cheek. Then Monika asked for me.

"What's up, Monika," I said.

"They want you too," she said to me.

"It's all good. I agree with Cheek. Do whatever you got to do, because I hear there are a lot of dudes back from the joint to testify against us anyway," I said.

After talking to Monika, Cheek and I hopped into his pearl white Maxima and turned a few corners. We discussed the conversation with Monika. I remembered something from our childhood, "Bro, remember that show that we use to watch as kids called Barretta? Remember what his saying was . . . if you can't do the time, don't do the crime! It's all good bro."

"Woo Daddy, I know it was going to come to an end one day, I just didn't know when. I guess we'll have to pay the piper soon," said Cheek.

Meanwhile, my gambling habit or addiction had gotten worse since I no longer had a job and had thoughts of prison on my mind. Now, just in case you are trying to figure out whether I had a habit or addiction, I will share the definition of habit and addiction with you. A habit is an acquired pattern of behavior that becomes customary practice or use. I once heard someone say—anything that an individual do for twenty one days becomes a habit. On the other hand, and addiction is a dependence or need of something. Therefore I would have to say conclude that I had a gambling habit, not an addiction. But I do believe that habits and addictions are interchangeable words.

Nevertheless, there's no way that I could ever get back all the things that my habit or addiction took from me. All I can do now is ponder on who I would be or where i could be in life if it wasn't for my habit or addiction.

As for my drug dealing lifestyle, nobody ever told me that the streets had an expiration date, and that drugs had no future. There's only two choices: Death and Prison! I'm now very much aware of my choice, which turned out to be prison. Around this time I was doing a lot of self thinking, talking to myself. "It just might be a good thing for me when the Feds come and get me. At least I want have to keep looking over my shoulder and my parents will no longer have to worry about me, and they'll know my whereabouts," I said to myself.

CHAPTER 9

THE INDICTMENT

On November 6, 1995 around six p.m., while on my way to the crib from an interview with Hardee's Restaurant, I was pulled over by a county cop. The cop came up on the passenger side of my car then looked into the backseat.

He then made his way to the driver's side and said, "Hello Mr. Joiner, how are you today."

"I'm just, fine, officer."

"Mr. Joiner, I stopped you because your license is suspended, but today is your lucky day. You may go." I said to myself how strange this incident was as I was pulling off. I tuned my music back up and continued my drive to the crib. As I turned into my neighborhood, a guy that I knew by the name of Ced stopped me. While I was talking with Ced, a city cop that I knew called me.

"Lynard, can I talk to you for a minute," asked the cop?

"Sure. but you must come up here," I replied. My reason for telling him to come where I was, is because, you never want anybody to see you talking to a cop without a witness or else people will think you're a snitch. Then they will rub your name in the mud all in the streets. Now. a snitch is an individual who gives information to the police about a crime that is being committed or have been committed. In jail, or prison they may also be called rats.

As the cop approached me he said, "Lynard there's a warrant out for your arrest for missing court on the twenty seventh of last month."

"That is not true" I responded. I went to court and my license is not suspended."

"Okay Lynard, you may be right, but I must place you under arrest for now. I'm going to take you downtown and if there's no warrant for you then you you will be free to go," he said. Believe it or not the cop laced me in the squad car without handcuffing me. The fact that he failed to handcuff me, I felt that it was certainly a mistake about the warrant. After I was there for about forty five minutes, they told me that they didn't have a warrant for me. The cop then told me that he must also take me to the county jail to see if they had a warrant to me.

As we left the City Jail, I noticed that we went past the county jail, but I didn't think nothing of it because the young lady who had joined him at the City Jail said that she was hungry. Once we got to Sixth Street, we turned down a dark alley. About a minute later I looked and seen a mail truck and said, "Kiss my wirist, the Feds got me."

"You're right, Lynard the Feds got you," said the officer. As we pulled up to the back of the old post office and stopped, a white man standing about 6'6" came out of the building. He immediately began yelling at the city cops because I wasn't handcuffed.

"This guy is listed as armed and dangerous," he shouted!

"He's not dangerous, said the male city cop. "I know him. "I'm going to write you up," the tall guy threatened.

"Well I guess he is dangerous. You all didn't go and get him, I did you a favor." The big white man was now red as fire in the face.

"You didn't do me a favor! I'll deal with you later!" You may be wondering why I didn't take off running while they were arguing. Well, one reason is I was so dang shocked that the Feds had me, even though I knew they was coming soon. "Hi Mr. Joiner',' said the big angry white guy. "Do you know who I am?" I didn't bother to respond. I just looked at him. Then he told me his name and position. "My name is Mr. Holloway and I'm with the U.S. Marshalls. You're getting ready to go to prison for a long time. You are being charged with conspiracy to distribute cocaine and crack cocaine . . . and we are not the state system." I still didn't say anything to him. He then took me inside of the building and took me to a small room. Once we got into the room, Agent Holloway said, "Would you like to help yourself?"

"How can I do that," I asked?

"All you have to do is tell me who you are getting your cocaine from, other than your brother."

"Why are you asking me stuff that I already know," I replied?

"Mr. Joiner listen, you don't have a record. So why would you go to prison when you don't have to go or at least you want go for a long time.

Mr. Joiner, I'm about to go and round up your whole family, and we are going to have a family reunion with you all." A few minutes later, an agent that I knew walked in.

"Hi Lynard, do you remember me," he asked? My name is Detective John Doe.

I remember you from your father's house when we raided it several times. I am here to help you save yourself. They told me that you are not in serious trouble. They just want you to tell them what role you played in the conspiracy"

"I don't know what you're talking about," I replied.

"Lynard, don't do this to yourself and your children. I promised you that the rest of them are going to get on the front seat of the bus, which means that they are going to help themselves at the first opportunity they get, and you will be left holding the bag as if you were the leader or some real bad guy. Lynard please think about it before it's to late. Take care of yourself."

After Mr. John Doe left, Mr. Holloway came back into the room.

"Would you like something to eat from McDonald's," asked Agent Holloway?

, I reached into my pocket and pulled out a wad of money and gave him a ten dollar bill. "You had better keep that for yourself," he said. "You're going to need it." I just gave him a half-hearted smile.

"Let me get a Big Mac, large fries, and a large coke."

"Would you like anything else? I mean it's going to be a long time before you see anymore McDonald's."

"Thank you, sir, but I've ordered enough."

They took me to a cell with a concrete slab in it. A few minutes later I was given a bed roll. I grabbed the bed roll and made the concrete slab as comfortable as I could make it, then I lie down. I guess another twenty minutes later, a young white man brought me the McDonald's I had ordered to my cell. As the guy walked away he said, "You will have some family company in about fifteen minutes. Just as the young Marshall said that, they began to bring several of my family members in one by one. The first one theybrouhgt in was my brother who we called The Mississippi Kid. About ten minutes later, ithey came in with my cousin, Mike P's. A few minutes later they showed up with my nephew, Lil-B.

A half hour later the U. S. Marshall came by the cell and said, "Guess what? We got your cousin Jason, his friend Bug, and the main connect, Mr. kandy-man.

Lynard, we will be back soon with the other two leaders. We will try our best not to harm them, but we know that they are the two most dangerous individuals in the Mississippi All Star Posse." About an hour later, the Marshalls came in with my brother, Cheek. Shortly after that, a Marshall came over to my cell and said, "Guess who we caught in the bed? Ganster D."

Then they put us all in the same cell and said, Y'all need to be together so that you all can get your story together, but y'all crack world is over.

Have fun."

CHAPTER 10

COUNTY JAILS

After being downstairs in the booking and receiving holding cell, an officer came by my cell saying, "Joiner! Get ready, you're going up stairs to J-Block." As I got upstairs to the door that served as the entrance to JBlock, several of the homies from the John Hayes Homes was banging on the window and shouting my name, Woo Daddy. Once the guard working control popped the door and I walked into the block, dudes was all in my business . . .

"The Feds got you too, huh," they inquired?

Moments later my baby-mom Red's brother came out of his cell saying, "What's up brother-n-law," he said.

"Nothing man. The Feds got a nigga," I replied. We went into his cell and that's when he gave me the 4-1-1 that was floating around the jail about me and the family. Just as my guy, T-Gram told Ke-bey, told me the exact same thing.

"Bro-n-law," he said. "There's so many suckers back here from the joint to testify against y' all that I can't even count them. That lame chump Stutter-Man, Black J, and your guy Donut is here. I seen these three wimps in the gym. I asked them what they were doing back at the county jail. They told me that they really didn't know why thay were back."

Now, whenever a dude came back to the county jail from the joint and tell you that he doesn't know shat he's back there for, then nine times out of ten, he is there to snitch on somebody or testify against somebody for the government, so that he can get a reduction in his sentence.

"What's up with you ke-bey? What are you doing here," I asked?

"The Feds got me too man. They charged me with three sales to an undercover cop. Now they want me to take an eighty seven month deal," said Ke-bey.

"That's seven years and three months," I replied.

"L.J., these people are knocking niggas heads off, even on a plea deal for crack. It's like getting sentenced for murder. I remember those Jones boys from Brown Street? They all are looking at life and the government really don't have evidence against them. Their attorney told them that since they are charged with conspiracy, the government really don't need any evidence.

All they need is two or three people to say the same thing about you," said Ke-bey. A week after being upstairs in the county jail, the guard came by my cell and spoke to me.

"Joiner," said the guard. "Get ready, the chain gang is coming to get you." I jumped up and washed my face and brushed my teeth. Then I sat back down on my bunk. I was asking myself—" Who in the heck is the chain gang.

I hope they know that we're not in slavery anymore."

A few minutes later, a guard came and took me down to booking and receiving. Once I got downstairs, I seen my co-defendant, Monika. I ran over to her and gave her a hug. The guard had something to say about that . . .

Joiner, you're not allowed to be around her, he said.

"This is my sister-n-law," I replied. "There's no problem with us." Now, just in case you're wondering what a co-defendant is: A co-defendant is a person that's charged on your case with you. After talking with Monika for about twenty minutes, the guard called me into a small office and hit me with some surprising news.

"The reason that I told you that you wasn't allowed to be around her is because she is a government witness against you and your family, but you didn't hear this for me," he emphasized.

Shortly after the guard got finished talking to me, two big country built white men came through the door with a handful of chains and handcuffs. Not thinking I began to speak out loud.

"Those must be the damn chain gang guys?" What they really were, was the U. S. Marshalls who transported you to the never ending chain of county jails.

You'd literally go from one county jail to the next, and to court. The chain gang told the eight of us t line up along the wall and face them. After searching us, one of them placed a chain around each one of our waist with a pair of handcuffs connected, which he put on our wrists. The other Marshall put a set of cuffs around our ankle which was connected by a short chain. Once we were all shackled, the two Marshalls escorted us to a white van. At this time, I felt like a run away slave who had been caught by his master. About three hours later, we was cruising down Seventy First Street and West Van Bureau in downtown Chicago. As we pulled up to the front of the high-rise building, an officer who was standing outside of the building pushed a button. A large garage door slowly began to rise up to the ceiling and we rolled into the parking lot. Once we got out of the van, we walked through several doors to the receiving and booking area. When we got to the booking area, a young lady came out and took Monika and Darla with her. This would be the last time I saw Monika.

After being in the holding cell for about fifteen minutes, a prison guard came around with a food cart yelling, "Chow time!" He gave each one of us a hot tray and a cold tray. The hot tray contained two hot dogs, baked beans and corn. I the cold tray, there was a handful of lettuce, two small salad dressing packs, two fruit punch kool-aid packs, two mustard and ketchup packs, along with a plastic spoon, and fork with a pack of salt and pepper inside.

Once we were done with chow, I experienced the most humiliating experience that a man can experience. I was told to strip naked in front of the guards. One of them stood directly in front of me and told me to raise my testicles.

Then he told me to turn around and raise my feet so that he could see the bottom of them. On top of this, now he told me to bend over, spread my cheeks and cough! I said to myself that they must be some undercover fags in order to do this job. I had never felt so violated in my life.

They threw each of us an orange jump suit with B.O.P. on the back of them. Of course the B.O.P. stood for Bureau of Prison. I was fingerprinted, photographed, and told to go see the nurse. Then after being booked in, a guard took me to meet my case worker. As I walked into her office, she told me to have a seat and she started asking me questions: "Did you or are you going to assist the government? Do you have any separtise? Do you have any family members that work here? Do you want to be in protective custody (PC) or general population?" I told Ms. White that I wasn't scared and that I wanted to be in general population. floor in general population."

"Okay then, you'll be on the thirteenth The floor contained two man cells, a dining area, a small kitchen, pool tables and two vending machines. There was also three small T. V. rooms and a small room with about three typewriters in it. My cell had a bunk bed, a small desk with a small over head light for reading and writing. The floor was made of tile and the walls were made of plain white concrete brick. My cell mate was an African guy named Crazy Barry. He was actually a nice guy.

He was facing fifteen years on a heroin case. I threw my bedroll on the top bunk and grabbed a chair, then I made my bed up. Barry and I began to talk and feel each other out.

"Where are you from," I asked?

"I'm originally from Miami," he answered. "But I caught my case on a hum bug. What are you here for?"

"They got me on a crack cocaine conspiracy. They claim that they bought crack from me three times. My attorney told me that she is going to look into my case further."

"Damn man," said Barry. "Is this your first time serving time?"

"Yes, but I did a few days in the county jail before." Then I asked him, "how long have you been at this place?"

"I've been here for two months man. "Do your family come and see you," I asked?

"Nah man, my family thinks that I'm a loser," he said.

"So when do we go to the commissary or the store around here? The food around here sucks, especially if it's all like what I had earlier."

"Hold on man, you just got here today. You can't complain. The food is damn good to me. They may not always have what I like, but I always like what they have," he joked. Now that got a serious laugh out of me. I actually laughed myself to tears. He waited on me to finish laughing before answering my question. "To answer your question, we go to commissary every Wednesday, but you must turn your commissary sheet in on Tuesday. Oh yea, you can have thirty dollars in coins, two rolls of quarters, and two rolls of dimes to buy stuff from the vending machines. Do you gamble? If you do, these dudes gamble like crazy after the ten o'clock count."

"Gambling is my thing, man. I'm going to make sure that I order that thirty dollars in coins."

"L.J., you never heard about the Feds? They take good care of you," he said. After kickin it with my cellie, I began to wind down for the night after the long day of drama. A few minutes later, a guard came through yelling count time. He repeated himself a few times to make sure we all heard him.

The next day after lunch, my cellie and I picked back up on our conversation about the Feds. Incase you're wondering, cellie is short for cell mate.

"L.J., it's a blessing to be in the federal system. The only bad thing about being in the federal system is they don't give you conjugal visits, and they no longer have parole."

"So do they expect you to do all of your time without getting any pussy? They got to be crazy."

"The only way that you will get that is to catch the right guard in the visitation room and pay them a hundred bucks to let you take your girl in the men's bathroom for a few minutes," said Barry. L. J., they take count time very serious around here. You got a twelve noon count Monday thru Friday. You have a four p.m. count everyday, which is the most important count of the day, because they must report the count in to Washington D.C."

"I guess this is the way that Uncle Sam keeps up with his legal slaves," I said.

"Yea, they also have a three a.m. count and a five a.m. count, said Barry. "If you're not where you're supposed to be at count time, they will write you an incident report for being out of bounds, and might put you in the S.H.U. Special Housing Unit, or the hole., especially during four o'clock count." While talking to my cellie, my case worker called me to her office and told me that I could now use the telephone. I immediately went and called my mom and stepfather to let them know that I was okay, and not to worry. My mom was the one to answer the phone.

"Hello moms, how are you doing?"

"I'm okay, baby. How are you doing," she replied?

"I'm okay moms, I just wanted to make sure that you and Pops was are okay. I'm in Chicago. They're going to take me back to Springfield in a couple of weeks. Oh yea, I don't need any money, I had a few hundred bucks in my pocket when they picked me up. Hey mom I have to get off the phone now, but I'll call you back in a few days."

"Okay baby, I will tell your Pops that you said hello. Baby I want you to get you a Bible and read chapter eight of the book of Romans, verses thirty one through thirty nine. Pops and I are here for you and we are praying for you. I love you. Bye." After getting off of the phone with my mother, I went into my cell and climbed into my bunk. I broke down crying with my face toward the wall just in case my cellie walked in, he wouldn't see me crying.

A week later, I moved up to the seventeenth floor. As I walked through the door, I heard a couple of people calling my name. It was two of my homies from the John Hay Homes Projects, C.W. and Red. The two of them took me into their cell and we talked for about an hour. They asked me was there anything that I needed and they told me that they had it going on on this floor.

"I'm good for now," I told them. "I just went to the store a few days ago." C. W. spoke up about how they had heard that the Feds had arrested me and my family. "You remember Lebron's wife named Alisha, who got caught up in 1993 in that Jack sting operation? She wore a wire on us. I just left Sagmon County Jail and there is all types of niggas from the joints waiting to testify against us."

"That's crazy, man. y' all was good to all of us out there. I seen Monika downstairs last week in medical," said Red. Now, after talking "'ith the homies for a while, the counselor called me into his office and gave me a handbook with all of the prison rules in it. He then assigned me to a cell, but my guy C.W. went into the office and spoke to the counselor. When he came out he told me that his guy, Ray had an empty bunk in his cell. Ray's cell was right next door to C. W. and Red, so that worked out conveniently for us. Once were in the cell, C.W. and Red told me about their case. They told me that Nelson had set them up at the Red Roof Inn. If you remember,

Nelson was one of the guys that showed me how to cook cocaine into crack. They also told me that J.B. wore a wire on them while buying a quarter kilo of crack from them. They was facing ten years to life just like me. After our talk, they introduced me to some of the guys that was in there. The first guy they introduced me to was Jessie Jackson's brother. Then I met several of the Gangster Disciples and Vice Lords. C.W. and Red gave me the run down on how things worked in MCC and how to stay sucker free. We shared our worries concerns and fears.

"It's that time of the day," yelled the young black officer who had just came through the door! Four O' clock count!" We all made our way to our cells.

While we were in the cell, Ray told me that Shorty was a cool guard and he knew him from the streets. About forty five minutes later, Shorty let us back out of the cell. "Chow time, chow time," yelled Shorty! That day we had fried chicken, corn, mashed potatoes with gravy, mac and cheese, and dinner rolls.

Minutes later the two inmates that was serving the good called us back up to the kitchen window and gave us a cold tray. The cold tray had a salad, strawberry jello, a dinner roll, and two packs of grape kool-aid. I guess the cooks downstairs made a mistake and put the dinner rolls in the hot tray, but it was okay with me because I was as hungry as a roaring lion. I knew this was the last meal for the day, until six o'clock the next morning.

Six a.m. rolled around and the guard came around yelling for chow. The doors opened. I decided to lay in my bunk for about ten minutes while my cellie got himself together because the cell wasn't big enough for both of us to move around at the same time. After my cellie, Ray finished getting himself together, then I got up and got myself together.

As I exited my cell I saw that the chow line was very long. Most of the inmates were related to Fire Marshall Bill . . . in other words they jumped straight up out of their bunks and got in the chow line without washing their face or brushing their teeth. The bad thing about these Fire Marshall Bill types, is that they want to talk to you with that morning breath kicking like Bruce Lee. They served pancakes, bacon, oatmeal, banana, and milk. I went and sat at the back of the dining room where all of the brothers ate.

After breakfast was over, I went back to my bunk and chilled out. About thirty minutes later the guard called me to his office and told me to pack out, I was leaving for court. After leaving the guard's office, I went and woke up my homies to let them know that I was leaving. C.W. and Red jumped up when I knocked on their door.

"What's up L.J., you okay," asked C.W.?

"I just stopped by to let y'all know that I'm getting ready to go and get my time," I replied.

"You're in my prayers," said Red. I gave Red and C. W. about fifteen dollars in coins and all of my commissary.

Once I got downstairs to R & D, they told me that the U.S. Marshalls was on their way to get me. One of the guards took me in the back and tossed me an orange jumpsuit with that big ugly B.O.P. stamp on the back of it. While waiting for the guard to take me through the humiliating strip routine, I was just standing there in nothing but my boxers. "Joiner, what are you waiting on to get dressed? I don't want to see your black naked ass," said the guard.

Once I got dressed, he took me to the holding tank where three other inmates were. They were from Peoria, Illinois. All three of them knew my niece Lizzie who lived in Peoria. About ten minutes later, the chain gang came through the door. As we got shackled, the U.S. Marshall told us that we was going back to the county jail for court. Then we were escorted in the van.

After stopping at the Peoria County Jail and dropping the three guys off, one of the Marshalls said to me, Joiner, I followed you several times, because we had so many addresses on you. We just wanted to know where to find you." I just laughed. An hour later, we pulled up into the Bangman County Jail garage. The county jail officer immediately booked me in and sent me upstairs r to K-Block. As I got upstairs and walked past J and L Block, I saw a couple of guys that I knew that was in the joint. Some were on dope charges. One of the guys was my so called right hand man, Donut, and the other guy was Twan.

I made eye contact with Donut and he immediately dropped his head. Once the K-Block door came open, I walked into the block and threw my bedroll in my cell, then came back out into the day room area.

"My nigga, Woo Daddy," I heard a voice call. "What's happening?" I looked around and didn't see anyone. "Up here Woo Daddy," the voice called again.

I looked up and saw my guy, Brian. Then I went to the top floor and kicked it with him.

"What are you in here for," I asked?

"I'm doing sixty days on a weed case, because I missed my court date, he replied.

"I know you already have the run down on us," I said. Brian laughed.

"You niggas is the talk of the town and here in the county jail Every nigga and his mama is talking about getting a time cut for testifying on you niggas."

"That's crazy, man. These chumps ain't about nothing. They can't even carry their own weight," I said. After discussing our case, Brian and I began to reminisce about the streets and our past. The first thing that I reminded

Brian of was when a girl named Gloria robbed him while they were getting busy.

"L.J. you're wrong for bringing that up, but I got a good one for you."

"You think so, I bet you don't," I dared.

"You remember that time when your baby mama Red played Jason on your rental car with that axe?"

"Boy, that's a darn good one," I replied. After kicking the bo—bo about three hours, the chow wagon came around. We had meat loaf, green beans, mashed potatoes, gravy, bread, and cookies. I must admit that it was good or either I was hungry_ The guard came back with some grape kool-aide_ I didn't have a cup so Brian gave me a peanut butter jar. Once we finished eating, we went and watched my favorite television show, "In The Heat Of The Night."

Then we turned to the news once that went off. The first thing the news reporter said was, "A high ranking gang member from Chicago has agreed to cooperate with the federal government in the Joiner case." All I could do was look on in disbelief. Brian asked me why didn't they give his name and if I knew who he was?

"I know exactly who he is," I said. Once the news went off, Brian and me went into my cell and played casino until the guard yelled for lock down.

As soon as the doors came open around six a.m., Brian came to my cell and said, L J., sleep late and you will lose weight."

"I'm on my way out, just as soon as I get myself together." I finally came out of the cell and got in line. When I got to the door and reached through the chuck-hole in the door, I looked up and saw my guy Country Mo, he was serving the meal as a trustee. There was french toast, sausage, grits, a banana, and frosted flakes with milk. I gave Brian my sausage for his banana, because it was pork. Just for the record, I'm not Muslim, I'm a Christian who don't have a holy than thou attitude.

While heading back to my cell after breakfast, the officer called me to the bubble window and told me to bunk and junk, the chain gang was on their way to take me to Petersburg County Jail. I ran upstairs to Brian's cell to let him know that I were leaving. Brian got up and gave me a man hug "LJ., you're a good guy, man. Keep your head up, God will make a way," he said.

Thanks B's stay focussed and sucker free. Once I got downstairs the guard patted me down and placed me in the booking cell. There were a couple of guys in the cell that I knew from the hood, They told me that they were being held on a trespassing charge from the John Hay Homes. The way that worked is, if you got three write ups in the projects for any type of violation, you was not allowed to be in the projects for sixty days. After kicking it with the guys for a few minutes, the chain gang came through the door. It was the same two Marshalls that had dropped me off the day before.

The Marshalls went up to the desk and signed a couple of papers. Then they placed me in shackles and we headed to the Petersburg County Jail.

As we pulled up to the jail and saw how small it was, it reminded me of the Mayberry County Jail on the Andy Griffin Show. Once I walked into the jail, there was a young white boy with a two piece orange trustee uniform on.

Once he heard that my name was Joiner, he went to the back of the jail.

Moments later, I heard my brother, Cheek and my nephew yelling my name.

"Woo Daddy, what's up boy It's about time you made it here," they said.

It felt kind of like a mini family reunion as the lady guard walked me to the cell. I was placed in a three man cell with Cheek and my nephew. It was my first time seeing them since our arrest. We talked and laughed all night, then slept all day the next day. The only time that we got up was to eat and shower. There was no kitchen inside this jail, so all of the food was ordered from a catering company nearby. That worked out well for us, because the food was excellent, we ate like kings in that jail.

Cheek introduced me to all of the guards in the jail. There was an old man named Murphy who worked from midnight to eight a.m. Murphy would let us watch T.V. until three a.m., now that was cool. We had cable: Showtime, HBO, MTV, and BET. We even had a remote control in our cell, and there was a T. V. in front of every cell.

Ms. Pat would bring us good movies to watch. Most of them would be new releases. Believe it or not, we even got to see pay-per-view fights and wrestling. The food was so good and the portions was nice, you really didn't need any commissary. On the other hand, we were able to order commissary on every Tuesday, but if you ran out of something and they had it on hand, they would allow you to buy it. We were able to buy soda from eleven a.m until lockdown, seven days a week.

During visitation, our family would bring us a home cooked meal, and the trustee would go out to the car with our relatives and get the food and bring it back to our cell in a trash bag. We would feed him good and throw him a few dollars for the favor.

On Halloween Night, the Chief of Police gave each one of us in the jail a large bag of assorted candy. The crazy thing about Halloween that night, we could hear the children when they came into the jail yelling trick or treat. I must admit that it was very nice of the jail to do that for the children in the community.

On Christmas, they allowed our family to bring us a home cooked plate of food. We didn't have to sneak it in. There was not a day or night that passed by that I didn't read my Bible and pray to God. I began to have conversations with God on a regular basis. The Lord is the only one that could help me. I held the scripture in chapter eight of Romans and verse thirty-one close to my heart. It read: "If God be for me, who can be against me?"

My brother, Cheek went to sentencing and they gave him twenty one years and sent him to MCC Chicago immediately. The only thing that I could say to him was, "Bro, God is in control, keep the faith." About two weeks before my sentencing, my attorney came to visit me and told me that I would probably receive a sentence somewhere in the area of ten years.

"Lynard., I will also look into asking them to send you to an institution that has a cooking school," she said. "I will send you a copy of the government's memorandum as soon as I get it. Take care and I'll see you at sentencing."

CHAPTER 11

THE DEATH SENTENCE

The night before my sentencing, I laid down in my bunk until about four a.m., just staring up at the ceiling in deep thought. I couldn't stop thinking about how I had made a choice to sell drugs which was about to place my life on hold for a long period of time. As I continued to stare at the ceiling, I began to think about the sentence that I was facing on tomorrow. I knew there would be no more shopping sprees, no more hopping from woman to woman, and no more V.I.P. image for me, because, I knew I'd be locked up for a long time. My conspiracy carried a penalty of ten to life. My eyes began to fill with water as the thought of not being able to be there for my children in the most critical stages of their lives ran through my mind.

As I rehearsed my drug selling run, I asked myself, "Were all of the money, women, cars, and the rest of the materialistic things worth the time that I was about to spend in prison? Was it worth me leaving my children and my family as a whole? HELL NO!!!" Even though I could never change what happened, and knew that I would never be able to give this time back to my children that I was about to rob them of, I said, "If I could turn back the hands of time, I would have done things different." Just before I fell asleep I felt a sense of peace come over me. "Lord, I am sick and tired of being sick and tired from all of the drama that the dope game has brought me," I said to myself. I just wanted a peace of mind again. A couple of hours later, the guard came around.

"Joiner, get up and get yourself together, said the guard. "The Marshalls will be here to take you to court. I will be back with you some breakfast." After eating breakfast and waiting on the Marshalls, I read my favorite verses from the book of Romans, chapter eight, verses thirty one through thirty nine, then I said a prayer. Shortly after praying, the Marshall showed up. Once I was shackled, we headed to the Federal Court House in Springfield, on Monroe Street. As I exited the transport van, making my way to the Federal

Building, all three T. V stations was on their way into the building. I made my way into the room before they could get set up.

My attorney, Ms. Deir showed up a few minutes later She told me to stay calm no matter what. She said that she knew that I had no problem speaking my mind, so that I s why she wanted me to be calm. I gave her my word that I would hold my peace as long as she didn I t let them railroad me. As my codefendants and I made our way into the courtroom, I made eye contact with my family and slowly walked over to the seat beside my attorney.

The Court: Good morning everyone. This is 95-77777, United States of America versus Lynard Joiner and Co-defendants. They have been convicted of count one of a ten count indictment, being conspiracy to distribute cocaine.

The government' witness list contained seventy six witnesses in order to convict the defendants.

The Court: Thank you. Let us now turn to Mr. Joiner. Mr. Joiner have you discussed your PSI and its contents with your attorney?

Mr. Joiner: Yes.

The Court: And at this time I will reflect on the record that you object to paragraph 425, which holds you accountable for 1.5 kilograms of cocaine base, crack.

The judge then overruled my objection to my drug amount and denied it even though the government did not present any solid evidence. He then denied my objections to being a manager or supervisor. Then the Judge asked my attorney did she have any objections to his findings.

Ms. Dier: No, your Honor.

Lynard we are going to be okay, she turned and said to me."

The Prosecutor: Cousel, your Honor, the guideline range for Mr. Joiner is 235 to 293 months. We are going to recommend the low end of the guideline range, because he has a criminal history of 1. I leaned over to my attorney and asked her, "What happened to a sentence in the area of ten years?" At that point my attorney stood up.

"Lynard is a family man, he has five children. None of the government's witnesses seem to agree on anything they said about Lynard," my attorney argued. "Lynard has a history of employment. Ever since he was fifteen years old, he has worked. There is no violence in his record. The only criminal activity in his record is one charge for unlawful possession in 1990, for which he got 1410 probation and no conviction was entered. Based on Lynard's past history of no violence, no prior criminal record, his family ties, his history of employment, and possibly his mental capacity from being in this circumstance which had stressed him out, I would like to see the court depart below the guidelines and give Lynard a chance to start his life over, away from his family, and everything else that got him into this in the first place. I would also ask the court to recommend that Lynard be placed at an institution, where they have a cooking school. He's been a cook for a long time, he would like to increase his ability in cooking," she continued to speak. "I would also recommend that he enter a drug rehabilitation program even though he doesn't have a history of drug misuse, if any at all. Thank you your Honor."

The Court: Now pursuant to the Sentencing Reform Act of 1984, and November 1, 1995, it is the judgement of this court that the defendant Lynard Joiner, is hereby committed to the custody of the Bureau of Prisons to be imprisoned for a term of 235 months, the lowest of the guideline range. No fine will be imposed.

As I looked back at my family, all of them had a look on their face like-I know he didn't just give L.J. two hundred and thirty five months. My family could not believe it!

"Don't worry Lynard, we're going to appeal it. I'm sorry," said my attorney. I took a deep breath and waited for the Marshalls to come and get me. As we headed out of the courtroom, I made eye contact with the prosecutor and the probation officer. While on the way back to the holding tank, my nephew's attorney asked the Marshall could he talk to me for a second. He told me . . . Lynard, whatever you do, please appeal your case they didn I t give you a fair sentencing trial. Take care of yourself." Once I got to the holding tank, the Marshalls had McDonald's waiting on us. With all the drama that I had been through in the last hour or two, food was definitely not on my mind. I did not have an appetite to eat at that time. I gave my co-defendants my food.

When I returned to the county jail, I went into my cell and had a long talk with God. "Lord, why me? I didn't kill nobody, I'm not a bad person. I looked out for people and never hurt anyone. Maybe I was wrong for selling drugs, but other people have done more wrong than I have and they didn't get as much time as me, I blamed everyone, but myself and I trie.d to plead my case to God About two weeks later, during breakfast, the guard told me that the Marshalls were coming to get me and my stay at Petersburg County Jail Pennhouse was over. I must admit, I could've cried when they told me that the Marshalls was there to get me. I hated to leave that county jail.

Once the Marshalls got there and shackled me, all of the county jail guards shook my hand again and told me to be good and take care of myself.

Finally, the Marshalls escorted me to the van and we headed for MCC Chicago.

They decided to drive down 11th Street instead of 9th Street to get on 55 North for whatever reason. I said to myself, "I guess he. wants me to have one last look at the John Hay Homes Projects, my old hustling ground, because it gave me an opportunity to face the image man face to face that me and other people had created through my lifestyle and an opportunity to die to my old self slowly.

CHAPTER 12

OXFORD WISCONSIN

My first prison flick after working out with cheek for about six months.

As we left MCC Chicago and made our way onto the freeway, all of enjoyed every minute of the ride, peering out at Lake Michigan. We were staring at all of the different vehicles and the people inside of them, especially the women. Some of the women even smiled and waved at us. Once we arrived in the city of Oxford, we passed a sign that said: Oxford Federal Correctional Institution ahead. About two miles beyond the sign the guard made a left onto a forest street. I noticed that the streets were named in alphabets. I thought to myself that this place must be in the middle of nowhere.

As we pulled up to the prison, several guards approached the bus with riffles. There were two on the side, one in the front and one in the back of the bus. A man wearing a white shirt and gold badge and name tag came onto the bus.

"Everybody, listen up," he said, making his presence felt. "When I call your name, come up here and give me your register number and follow the guard inside." While sitting on the bus looking at the shining razor wire I thought to myself . . .

"Oh Lord, I know this is not the place where I am going to spend the next twenty years of my life." The guard finally called my name. I made my way to the front walking like a penguin, because of the shackles. We then walked down a long hallway and two flights of stairs into the booking and receiving area.

After being processed in, we crossed the center of the compound on our way to the A&O building. That's where all of the new arrivals go until they are assigned to a housing unit. There was inmates standing everywhere watching us. When we turned the corner to go into the A&O building, there was dudes of all races trying to hand us a care package with a knife, saying, "You're going to need this too." None of us took the offer. Suddenly I heard someone calling my name.

"Woo Daddy! Over here, Woo Daddy! L.J.!" It was my so called cousin, D.J. There was also guys that I hadn't seen since I left the street as well as people I hadn't seen in a decade calling me. "Cheek told us that you was on your way here, cousin," said D.J. "He's at work right now, but we will come and see you after four O' clock count. Don't take nothing to nobody, we got you as soon as the count clear."

My cellie was a guy named Alphonso, but everybody called him St. Louis, because that was where he was from. He was a very cool brother with a great sense of humor. After we felt each other out and St. Louis gave me the rulesfor the room, I told him that I had no problem with them. He then asked me, "How much time do you have?"

"I got railroaded, a fresh nineteen years and seven months. What are you working with," I asked?

"I got about seven more to do on a fifteen piece," he replied. "I know you really don't know me, but whatever I got, you got. This is how we get down in this crib." I had never thought of prison as the crib, but it was now my place of residence, so it was true in a sense.

After kicking it with st. Louis, I made my bunk up and lie upon my bunk.

About five minutes later I heard the guard yelling "On your feet! Count time! La Cuenta! Count time! Cuenta!" He mixed the spanish in his announcement to so that the Latino inmates that didn't speak english could understand that it was count time.

Once the count was clear, Cheek and D.J. gave me a big bag of hygiene products, some sneakers, and a bag of zoom zooms and wam-wam. That was prison terminology for snacks and junk food. After I took the bag to my room and came back out, Cheek and D.J. gave me a tour of the yard. As we strolled the yard, I noticed that everyone was with their own race: whites with whites; blacks with blacks; native americans with each other; and Latinos with Latinos. All of them were just hanging out with their own, playing cards, dominos, basketball, tennis and musical instruments. Cheek and D.J. introduced me to all of the homies that was from Illinois. They were from East St. Louis, Decatur, Peoria, Champaign, Chicago, and Danville. We really didn't get along with each other on the street. But in the joint, we had to put our differences to the side because you posse up based on the state that you were from. There was all types of gangs on the yard such as Vice Lords, Gangster Disciples, Crips, and Bloods, Dirty White Boys, and several Mexican gangs.

After walking the yard for a couple of hours. I asked D me and Cheek for a minute so that we could talk in privacy. So we walked over to the east side of the yard away from everybody and sat upon a big rock that was on the yard. We hugged each other again.

"Bro, it's a blessing to see you and have you here with me," said Cheek.

"Bro., being in this placeis like being in another world in the army or somewhere. There are people here from all walks of life. Just as we were close out there, we must be even closer in here, because if these niggas see any sign of weakness in you, they will try you. L.J., I must tell you this . . . you see and don't see, hear and don't hear. Mind your own business and we are going to do our own time Bro. "Bet Bro., I replied. "We are going to do this together and take care of each other," I said.

"Oh yea Bro. I forgot to tell you to make sure that you don't let any

Cheek and me had each other back at all times.

of the homies send you off. Sometimes they get into stuff that they shouldn't be into, because one of their gang members buddies is having odds with some body. I tell them that I am not gang related, so that doesn't concern me. I don't care how they take it.

"Cool Bro., what is understood don't need to be explained. We are one at all times," I replied. At 8:30 p.m. they began to shut the yard down, so Cheek walked me back to my unit. While on the way back to the unit, I heard a guard say over the yard speaker . . .

"Get your meds from the Feds at this time."

"This is pill line for people who need medication to cope with this time in order to keep from going crazy or committing suicide," said Cheek.

"You remember that medicine that Ty use to take to keep him from being so hyper, there's people here on that stuff."

"I guess you got to do whatever it takes to do this time or it will do you."

"Bro, the only thing we have to do in here to make it is to trust God and take it day by day," said Cheek.

"Man, you're one hundred percent right, we are going to do it together day by day," I replied. "I would like to do my 235 months in one day, but it just don't work that way. I'll see you tomorrow."

When I got back to my cell, St. Louis asked me how did I know Cheek.

He said that Cheek was a good down to earth brother.

"Yea, he's my flesh and blood brother," I said.

"Now that I'm looking at you, you two do kind of look alike and y all also walk alike," replied St. Louis. Then he proceeded to show me his photo album which had a lot of girls in it. Most of the women in his photo album only had on their bra and panties, in all kinds of different provocative poses. I really didn't stare at them, because I didn't want him to think that I was fending on his chicks.

The next day after the four p.m. count was clear, Cheek and D.J. came to check on me. "Bro. I got a group of guys that I really want you to meet around six p.m. in the Chapel," said Cheek.

"Bet," I agreed! "I can't wait to see them." Then we walked to the Chow Hall to grab a bite to eat. They were serving grill cheese, chili, fries, chocolate, and soda. The chow line was very long on both sides.

"Let's go on the black side," said Cheek.

"What do you mean by the—black side," I asked. I didn't give Cheek time to answer . . . "Never mind, I see what you mean now by saying the black side." The Chow Hall was as segregated as the yard was. There were guards watching the chow line to make sure that you didn't get extra food. Now there was rice, beans and soup on the Hot Bar. You could get as much as you wanted from the Hot Bar.

"L.J., be very careful when you come into this kitchen, because at any given minute a fight may break out," said D.J. We made our way to a table in the back with the rest of the black brothers. A young white guy came over and joined us. After looking around in the Chow Hall, I felt somewhat uncomfortable with the white boy sitting at the table with us. Not that I'm prejudice, but I was told that the whites and blacks have nothing in common unless it's concerning business. I saw a bunch of white dudes talking amongst themselves. I kept looking at them out of the corner of my eye. Cheek must have read my mind, because he tapped me on my shoulder.

"It's okay, n said Cheek. "Everybody knows that Brad hangs out with us.

His girlfriend is black." I must admit that I was always on the defensive side, based on my television view of prison. My motto was—If you stay ready, you don't have to get ready. As we finished up and walked to the kitchen window to put away our trays, I heard somebody calling me.

"Hey L.J., what's up boy? When did you get here?" It was Tommy-T, he was Cheek's wife's uncle.

"I got here yesterday around three p.m.,". I answered.

Then Tommy-T said to Cheek, "why didn't you bring Woo Daddy to see me last night?"

"Uncle, to be for real, I forgot," said Cheek. "I was so glad to see him. We will swing by to see you after we get out of church." We walked on over to the Chapel and watched a couple of videos featuring the Mississippi Mass Choir. My favorite gospel song was on one of the videos: "Near The Cross."

Six o'clock rolled around and Cheek turned the video off and we got up and went into a room, toward the back there was about eight guys sitting in the room with bibles. Once inside, Cheek introduced me to all of the guys.

"This is Brad, Steve, Vick, Joe, Mosely, Stacey, and Boston," said Cheek.

"What's up guys," I said. They were all Christians, and by my family household rule, I too was a Christian. I really didn't know anything about the Bible for real. I only knew three books in the Bible: Job, psalm and corinthians. I learned about the book of Corinthians while I was in the street messing with this devil in disguise girl named Rose. She tried to act all holy, but she was an undercover unrepented Rahab. I thought the book of Job was pronounced like a job, place of work. I also thought the book of Psalms was pronounced like a palm tree. There were several other religions such as two separate groups of Muslims, Catholic, Buddhist, Jehoval Witnesses, and the Hebrews. Now, to keep it real, some guys in prison hide behind religion or use it as a crutch. In other words, they fake it to make it. This is just a reality for a lot of people that are in prison. As you continue to read this book, you may say the same about me, or worse. I will make it very clear that I still don't have all of my I' s dotted, nor do I have all of my T's crossed, but I promise you that I am striving day by day to be a better man, person, father, and son, but most of all to be a man of God after his own heart. In other words, I am a work in progress.

Even though I was a Christian, there was other groups trying to recruit me. My homeboy, Abraham X was trying to get me to become a Muslim. He would tell me stuff like, the white man is a blue eyed devil, and the Bible has been tampered with by the white man's god.

I immediately told him, "Abraham, I'm not with that mess, I am a Christian and I am going to die as a Christian." Abraham X was a soldier in the Nation of Islam, but I knew him from the hood, and he never said anything about being a Muslim.

About two weeks later, Abraham, said, "I can respect what you believe, even though I disagree with it, but I want you to come over to the Chapel on Friday at two p.m. and hear me speak," he said.

"You got that, I'll be there, but you must go to church with me Sunday."

I really didn't want to go and listen to Abraham talk about the white man and what they have done to us. The Nation of Islam guys blamed the white man for all of the black man's issues and problems.

That Friday I went over to hear Abraham X lecture. He was the acting minister since John X had been thrown in the hole for cursing the teacher out. As I got into the Chapel, all of the brother X's greeted me. As Abraham X started preaching, he asked a question" "Why do you think that after four hundred years, we are still oppressed, broke, in bondage, depressed, and trapped in the unjust prison system? If you say, because of the white man, you're right. They are the devil with those blue eyes." All of the guys stood up and clapped their hands. Abraham X continued talking. "I don't know why my Christian brother continue to believe in the white man's god. If Jesus love them so much, who do they think is God. Why do he allow these white folks, blue eyed devils to take us away from our family, homes, and communities. And they shut us up in these prisons with long unjust sentences." While he was preaching, I was saying to myself that God didn't put us here, our choices put us here. I really didn't understand the whole God is Jesus, Jesus is God thing at this time. "The black man was on earth before any other race," said Abraham X. "The black man is very intelligent and powerful. This is why the white man is trying to kill us with that poison pork that they are serving over there in the Chow Hall. We must learn how to eat to live instead of living to eat." All of the brothers stood up.

"Yes:;, sir, black man," said the crown of brothers. While they were all on their feet hollering, yes sir black man, I was thinking about those thin cut pork chops that I use to fry, brown gravy, mac and cheese, green beans, and those flaky Hungry Jack biscuits that I loved. In order to make a long story short, Abraham X could've talked about the pig being poison until he was blue in the face, because I wasn't about to stop eating the pig. There was also a phrase going around that said—"if you want to get big, you must eat the pig." After preaching a little more hate on the white man, Abraham X asked us to stand for prayer. There was about one hundred and fifty brothers in there. I didn't close my eyes because I wanted to see what they were doing. They held their hands palms up like they were opening a book and said . . . In the name of allah the most merciful, I bear witness that there is no god but allah."

After the 'hate the white man' service was over, Abraham X said, "Thanks for coming, I see that you are still a man of your word."

I answered out of sarcasm, "Yes sir, I'm glad that I came too. I learned a lot about our people, the black man." Then he handed me their favorite book:

"Message To The Black Man" by the most honorable Elijah Muhumma. The only thing that I can say about Abraham X's racial teachings did for me was, it kept me focus on the only religion that I was taught and exposed to which was Christianity.

After a month and a half had gone by, I felt a little more comfortable in the prison world. I seemed like I was in another world with people from several different countries. Dudes would sit around all day reminiscing about the streets and his girl. At about 9:30 p.m., niggas would rush to the phone to call their girls before the 10 p.m. lock down. I really didn't like calling my girlfriend after eight O' clock, just in case 'Jody' had stopped by and I would never call early in the morning just in case 'Jody' spent the night.

Jody is the guy that is having sex with your girl while you are in prison.

He may be a family member, your so called best friend or even one of your enemies that you had on the street. An old man named J. J. dropped some knowledge on me one day.

"Never ask your girl where she was or is she screwing around with somebody," said J.J. "Because these are questions that will break your heart once she decide to come clean with you. Always give her a way out, especially if she is putting money on your books, writing you, and accepting your calls."

A few days later I was moved from the A&O unit to the gang banging unit:

Porhouse. My cellie in my new unit was an old hit man named, Mr. Camp. He was about fifty five years old and had done about twenty five years, and he still had about fifteen more to do. The time had gotten the best of Mr. Camp. He would sleep ready-to-roll every night. He kept his bags packed as if he was expecting an immediate release any day. All of the guys use to ask me how in the world do I live with that crazy man.

"I only sleep in there. By the time I go to bed he is sleep," I would say. I stayed in the room with Mr. Camp for a week and my counselor moved me up the hill to Marquette Unit with Cheek. We wasn't able to live in the cell together, because he was living with one of the Christian brothers. So I moved in the cell with a guy named Caveman.

I must say, Caveman was a perfect name for him. Not only did he have a Caveman stature, but he even lived like one! He would let the trash can run over before he emptied it. He would also leave his dishes dirty for days before washing them.

The Federal Prison system has six security levels, but you only hear about four of them: U.S. Penitentiary (USP), Medium, Low, Minimum (Camp). In the USP and medium institutions, you would prefer to sleep on the top bunk, because it is safer for you than the bottom bunk, just in case somebody try to run up on you in your cell and hit you. In other words, if you had beef with a nigga, and he was trying to sneak up on you, it would be a little harder for him to get you. One night around one a.m., a guy ran up into our cell and got in the bed with Caveman. I heard Caveman hollering.

"What are you doing in my bed with me!?"

"Shut up," said the other guy. "I'm sure not trying to rape your ugly ass. I just walked into the wrong cell." I just lie in bed faking sleep.

The next day I shared my experience with Cheek. He killed himself laughing at me.

"Why didn't you get up and help your cellie," asked Cheek.

"I didn't know if they were lovers or not, after I seen two dudes doing to another guy down the hill," I replied.

"I was just joking, bro," said Cheek. "You did the right thing." A week later Cheek and I began to work out together. He was much stronger that I was, so he was patient with me. After hitting the weights, we would walk about two miles. While walking the yard, Cheek and I talked about our relationship. I told Cheek that Evelyn broke bad on me two months after I got arrested, and I didn't know what to expect from Carissa. "Bro, the good thing about your relationship is at least you're not married to either of them," said Cheek.

"I don't know whether my wife is going to be able to stick it out with me or not, so I'm going to put crazy Kelli on my visitation list. If you do hook up with Carissa, be real careful about calling her early in the morning or late at night," Chee went on to say. "And don't ask her questions that you really don't want to hear the answer to."

The next day my counselor called me into his office and told me that he was giving me a job in the kitchen, based on a recommendation from the court that was in my paperwork. The next morning around four a.m., I was awakened by a guard with his flashlight shining in my face.

"Joiner," he said. "Food service wake up call. You got a half hour to be ready."

"Yes sir." I slowly got up and brushed my teeth, washed my face and got dressed. I made my way to the guard's office that was located at the front of the unit. Several guys including myself were escorted to the kitchen.

Once we got to the kitchen, we were greeted by the food service guard.

He had a medium build and his name was Casper. He gave us a tour of the kitchen and then assigned each one of us to a position. Since there was no openings to be a cook, I was assigned to serve on the line. A line server is the worst detail that you can have in the kitchen because the inmates and the guards both are sweating you about the food. The inmates want you to give them extra food even though the guards are telling you to only give one scoop of this and that, or only one of whatever is being served. Now, if you don't give one of the so called gangsters extra, you will have words or even have to fight him. Even though they know it's not your fault, they still attack you instead of the officer who's standing right there at the front of the line.

On chicken day, whether it's baked, BBQ'd, or fried, there would be two guards on the line. One would stand behind the line while the other one would stand in his usual spot at the front of the line. There would also be a guard in the dining room area watching for people trying to double-back. In prison, chicken is like steak . . . especially fried chicken. Even though the serving line is the most dangerous position in the kitchen, we got our kitchen hustling going by selling whatever was left over after last call. There was four of us on the line and we would split whatever we got. There times when we caught the guards slipping and we would hide a pan of chicken or hamburgers under the line or on the bottom of the warmer. Every now and then, the cooks would look out for us. The cooks would also take care of the guys in the pot and pans area washing dishes. They would bang those pots and pans out daily.

One of my homies worked in the bakery. He told me that all five of them had been there for over three years and the job was gravy. They made cookies, bear claws, doughnuts, twisters, long john, cakes, and pies. They also made special treats that never made it to the serving line, but you could by them out on the compound yard or in the units. The homie took good care of me and Cheek. In return, I would take care of the homie from the serving line. The guard allowed me to take care of Cheek as he came through the line by turning his head. Most of the guards would make sure that we ate better than the inmates who didn't work for the kitchen. We were allowed to take a couple of items out of the kitchen with us at the end of the shift.

Everyday there would be about twelve guys in the T.V. Room watching soap operas. They would watch Young and The Restless, One Life To Live, General Hospital, All My Children, and As The World Turns. I lived by the golden prison rule—never turn the T.V., and always sit with your back to the wall in case something jumped off. Since my off days were Saturday and Sunday, I would stay up and watch Midnight Love on BET. The T. V. Room would be packed with brothers glued to the T. V., watching the videos and trying to sing and dance to those slow jams. Once Midnight Love went off, all of the guys would jump up and run to the phone and call their girl with vaseline and a sock in their hand in hopes of having phone sex. Some of them would grab a picture of their girl and head to the shower to take care of themselves. They would be in the shower making love to their girl in their mind. I never took my girl picture to the shower, but I am guilty of masturbation. This was how guys relieved themselves, it was a whole lot better than fooling with another man in any shape, form or fashion.

After 12 midnight, the bathroom became the dope house, motel, and the hang out joint. Niggas would be in the bathroom smoking cigarettes dope and drinking. There would also be guys in the shower engaged in homosexual activity. They were nasty, and would leave doo-doo and blood in the shower.

Folks in prison forgot that they left their mom or maid at home. If you say something to the fool about cleaning up after themselves, they have something stupid to say back to you like . . . "I just live like this in here."

That's a lie! You don't come to prison and pick up these types of bad habits, they are already in you. The same principal applies when a chump say that he only mess with boys and punks in prison. That's a lie too! He was just an undercover gump in the free world as we call it in the joint In other words, in the prison's world everyone have a way of doing their own time and passing the days by. Some guys be into sports some into selling drugs, while others into using drugs, some guys into my old habit—gambling, and some guys into messing around with punks and gumps. One night I got up at around two in the morning to use the restroom, and there was three guys in the restroom getting busy. Now that was sickening! Two of the guys had the other guy bent over in between them. One was doing him in the mouth and the other one was doing him from the back. These fools acted like they was running a train on a woman. I thought to myself how disgusting it was and how God made Adam and Eve, not Adam and Steve.

I must admit that I was in violation of several of the prison rules such as the one about minding my own business, and see and don't see, and hear and don't hear.

I hated to go visitation and see a fagget dude with a woman, acting like he's a real nigga, when he know that he's a gump for real. Some of these guys were so messed up in the head, they believe it's cool to mess with another man. They have the nerve to call themselves pimps. The truth is that they are homosexuals. The bad thing about these gumps is that they get out of prison and go and give a sister HIV/AID After working in the kitchen for about two months as a line server, my supervisor moved me to the P.M. cook shift with him. My so called Uncle Tommy-T who worked the P.M. dish room gave me the run down on how things worked on this shift.

"Nephew, it's this nigga named Red Man, he runs the P.M. cook shift and the P.M. kitchen as a whole. He is cool with me. Everything goes through him and then to the other crew leaders.," said Tommy-T. There were four cooks on the P.M. shift.

The next day as I walked into the kitchen, all of the homeboys with the 025, 026, and 424 of the last three digits of the register number came over to speak with me.

"L.J., watch those niggas that you are about to work with. If they try anything, let us know and we will step to those fools. This is how Illinois boys roll in here," they said.

"Bet, but I'm good fellas," I replied. The 025, 026, and 424 represents which part of Illinois you was from. 025 represented the southern district of Illinois. 026 represented the middle district of Illinois, and 424 meant that you were from the northern district. We could also tell what state other inmates were from by the last three digits of their number. For example, If a guys last three digits is 112, I knew that he was from some part of California, 042 or 043 meant Mississippi, 052, 053 Or 054 stood for New York.

039 or 040 represented Michigan.

Kaster, who was a tall slim white prison cook supervisor called me and gave a brief overview about my job duties. He gave me a menu and asked me a question.

"Joiner, what can you cook on that menu?"

"All of it. This menu is very simple," I replied.

"Are you sure, Joiner?"

"No sir. I'm positive!" Some people tell me that when it comes to cooking, I am not cocky, I am confident. That's all it is. After looking at the menu, I was introduced to the cooks. The head cook was named Red Man.

There was Jimbo, Pete, and Fruit Cake who who all worked under Red Man. I could tell that those cooks didn't like me right from the start, because of the look that was on their facese as the guard told them that I was now on the cook shift with them. The guard took me into his office and told me that I would be earning twelve cents per hour since I didn't have a highschool diploma or GED. "I know this man didn't just say he was going to pay me no damn twelve cents per hour," I said to myself.

Here's a copy of the pay scale," he saod as he handed it to me. As I looked on the pay scale sheet, I noticed that there was five pay rates and they all were in CENTS: forty, thirty-one, twenty-three, seventeen, and twelve cents. There was also a maintenance pay of $5.25 per month. I thought to myself how this is slavery allover again. The next day at work, I was asked to make a pot of brown gravy for twelve hundred guys. Then Kaster walked me into the storage room to get the ingredients that I needed. I grabbed a bag of flour, two large cans of beef base, garlic salt, white pepper, and some butter out of the cooler. I stopped by vegetable prep and asked them to cut me four inch pan of chopped onion. The first thing that I did after I turned the big kettle on was, I made a roux. A roux is made of equal parts of flour and shortening but I like using butter. I let the roux cook for a few minutes and then I began to season the roux with the beef base, garlic salt, and white pepper. After allowing the seasoning roux to cook a few more minutes, I broke the roux down with a little water and some milk to keep it creamy. Then I reduced the heat and added the chopped onion and let the ingredients simmer for about ten minutes. Then I took the paddle and stirred the gravy around. It was creamy and good, there wasn't a single lump in it. I made about thirty gallons of gravy.

As time passed and I was constantly showing my cooking skills, all four cooks began tosomewhat hate on me. After finishing my tasks, I would go over and ask them if they needed my help for anything.

"Nope! I got this, player," they would always say.

"If you need some help just call on me." One day I pulled Red to the side. "Red, let me talk to you for a minute."

"What's up man," said Red?

"Red, I'm not here to try to take your job, or nobody else's job, I'm just here to help and I'm not trying to step on anybody's toes. There is no 'I' in team," I said. Then we shook hands in agreement.

A week later, a fight broke out between two inmate kitchen workers. A guy named Big Ace weighed about two hundred pounds and stood about 6'1", body slammed a dude named Pookie. Pookie only weighed a buck fifty. Big Ace claimed that Pookie had stole his pan of chicken that he had stolen out of, the warmer.

After being body slammed, Pookie just got up holding his back and walked out to the dining room. The next day we were all sitting in the dining room playing cards. Big Ace and three other guys were playing cards at the table next to me. A few minutes later, I seen Pookie get up and walk to the back of the kitchen. About twenty minutes later, Pookie came back out of the kitchen with an aluminum pitcher in his hand. I noticed that he was walking in my direction. He passed my table and eased behind Big Ace and dumped the hot liquid on top of his head. We instantly knew that it was hot grease! I could see Big Ace's skin peeling off of him as he jumped up and ran. He tried to run out of the door to medical, but the door was locked. The guard came running from the back of the kitchen to see what was going on. By this time Big Ace was lying on the floor by the door still screaming. The guard pressed his duece button. It wasn't long before officers swarmed the kitchen running in from every direction. By this time, Big Ace had taken off his shirt. As the guards bursted through the door, the kitchen officer had Big Ace against the wall. The other officers was looking like—where is the guy who did it?

We were all questioned, but everyone claimed that we didn't see the incident, because we were distracted by playing cards. They checked us for burns and cuts. This is called a body check.

About three days later, the guards came and got Pookie for assaulting another person. Since the kitchen guard didn't see it, and nobody spoke up at the time that it happened, this meant that Big Ace told or someone that was in the kitchen snitched by placing a note under one of the guard's door.

A month later during lunch with all of the staff being present in the kitchen, a guy walked into the Chow Hall with an aluminum mop ringer in his hand. He strolled over to the black section of the dining hall and hit a guy named Killer in the side of his head with it. Blood gushed everywhere as well as Killer's teeth. The guy dropped the mop ringer and walked up to the guards and put his hands behind his back. A couple of the guards walked him on over to the SHU. Remember the SHU is the jail inside of the prison where you went when you broke the prison's rules. In SHU or Special Housing Unit, you are separated from the general population. You are on 23/1. THis means that you are locked down for twenty-three hours and you come out of the cell for one hour per day. You can either go to recreation, use the phone or go to the law library. Being in the SHU remind you of when you were in the county j ail. You sleep during the day and stay up all night.

In the meantime and between time, all of my co-workers and I became cool and hustling partners Just like on the street, we had to put our differences aside and work together and realize that there's enough for all of us to get our kitchen hustle on. We made sure that each of us made a couple books of stamps a day. The stamps was the money on the compound. We would sell them in exchange for commissary or have the guys to ask their people to send the money to our accounts. At times, my kitchen hustling business would remind me of my hustling days in the streets but it wouldn t last long, because I would justify my action by saying, "I got to do what I got to do in here to survive, and plus they're slaving me in here, only paying me twelve cents per hour." Even though I was in prison, I still had the street mind set. The homies and I talked about the streets and money twenty four-seven.

At this point I felt that I was the same person that I was on the street. I had no sense of direction. I simply didn't know which way I wanted my life to go, nor did I know what I wanted in life A year later while lying in my bed, around two a.m., in the wee hours of the morning, my whole past life flashed before my eyes. In my mind I began to walk down a road but I wasn't familiar with anything that I saw. I thought to myself that I must be lost. I continued this walk in my mind, looking for a sign or something that I was familiar with. I came to a fork in the road.

I couldn't make up my mind on which way to go, so I just stood there for a while. Then I heard someone say—"follow me and you will be okay." Believe it or not, I still can't really explain what happened, but the one thing that I did understand, I was lost in life with no direction.

When I got off work the next day, I told Cheek that we needed to talk. r shared my experience or whatever it was. Anyway, I told him about it.

"Bro., this is a time of separation from everything and everybody, so that God can have our undivided attention," Cheek said.

"I know that God is trying to tell me something, but what," I replied?

"L.J., remember that saying—just hang on to God's unchanging hand."

"It's good that we have each other to lean on," I said.

During the meal on day, Cheek told me that he needed to talk with me immediately. As r got to the table he told me that he was being transferred to the RDAP Unit. "Congrajulations bro," I said! "Please stay focussed and complete the program. You will get a year knocked off of your sentence, plus six months in the halfway house." I signed up for the RDAP course, but I was denied because I wasn't a drug user, nor did I drink. Once Cheek completed the program, he was put in for a transfer to Yazoo, Mississippi. Before Cheek left, I made him a big nacho and a nice fruit salad. A few days later, he left, headed for Yazoo City. I felt like a part of me had left, which it did.

Just as we were close in the free world, we were even closer in prison. About a year later, Cheek and I were reunited for a short period of time.

CHAPTER 13

THE PRISON MERRY-GO-ROUND

After being in FCI Oxford, Wisconsin for over two years, I was recommended for a transfer to Yazoo City, Mississippi. A month later, an officer came to my cell around 5:30 a.m.

"Joiner, wrap 'em up," he said. "Get yourself together and come to my office once you are done." Before going to the guard's office, I woke up Red Man and Jimbo and told them that I was leaving. We'd exchanged contact information the night before. I got an opportunity to holler at my two Christian brothers, Joe and Steve. I didn't get to say good bye to all of my homeboys except the few that I seen in the Chow Hall while eating breakfast before getting on the bus. Since we all had at least fifteen years, I knew that some of us would bump into one another somewhere in the system. After eating breakfast, a couple of guards walked me and five other guys to R&D.

Like usual, they lined all six of us up along the wall and told us to strip naked. After bending over and coughing, they threw each of us a pair of pants and a white t-shirt, and told us to get dressed. The two officers that was working in R&D put shackles on us. Just in case that forgot what shackles are, they are chains with handcuffs that connect your wrists to your waist in front of you, and restraints on our feet. After being shackled down they loaded us on the bus. Once the bus pulled odd, a van trailed us to the highway and turned around. Old man Bob told me that they did it for security reasons, just in case someone was trying to high-jack the bus. I just laughed, like yea right. It had been a couple of years since I'd seen the free world.

As we made our way onto the freeway, headed for MCC Chicago, I just stared out of the window at the big trucks and all of the different cats and vans, and the people that were driving them. As we arrived at Mce Chicago, the BOP Guard called everybody's name except mine, and told the guys this is where they would be staying for a while. About a half hour later, the guards returned to the bus with about forty inmates. Then we drove on the way to Terre Haute, Indiana.

When we arrived in Terre Haute, we went to the airport and parked in back of it. I really didn't know why we were just sitting on the bus at the airport. I guess it was written all-over my face, because the guy that was sitting across from me said, U "We are waiting on the airplane~' At this time, I still didn't know that we were going to get on a plane. Keep in mind that at this time I had never been on a plane before. A few minutes later, this huge plane landed, as I watched from my window. The guard that was driving the bus went ahead and drove over to where the plane was. As I turned and looked out of my window, there were U. S. Marshalls and Police Officers, as well as BOP Guards standing around everywhere with their rifles in their hands. There was so much security that I said to myself, "The president must be on that plane with all of these cops. A few minutes later a couple of woman came onto the bus.

"Listen up! When I call your name, make your way to the front and give me your first name and your register number," he said. While waiting to hear my name, my stomach began to fill with butterflies and I became nervous, but I didn't show it, or at least I don't think I did. Finally she called my name and I made my way to the front of the bus.

"Lynard Joiner, 10642-026," I said.

"I just needed your first name," she said with a smile on her face. As I got off the bus and looked around, I couldn't believe the security and all of the other inmates that were standing out there. There must have been over a hundred cops and about thirty-five hundred inmates. There were approximately eight Marshalls checking us and telling us which bus to get onto, or to get in the planes line. I had never seen anything like it before in my entire life.

It looked like a modern day slave trade! It was as if the slave owners were swapping slaves, saying—"I'll take these over here and you take those over there." Once i got checked, I was told to get in the plane line.

Once we got on the plane, the Marshalls placed us in our seats. They put me right in the place where I didn't want to sit . . . by the window. All of the women sat up front, while us guys sat at the back of the plane. As the plane got ready to take off, I said a prayer, "Lord please take the wheel of this plane in your hands and guide us safely to our destination." I asked this prayer in the name of Jesus before saying Amen. While I was praying I heard the airplane pilot giving instructions. One we hit the runway and got up into the air, I felt a little better. A few minutes later the Marshalls gave each of us on the plane a brown bag lunch. Inside the bags was a cheese sandwich, bologna sandwich, cheese crackers, an apple, and a bag of juice. Since we had on shackles, we had to eat our food like animals, because the chains were so short that we could not extend our arms.

After about three hours, it felt like the plane was falling out of the sky, so I slowly turned and looked out of the window, only to find out that the plane was getting lower because we had reached Oklahoma City, Oklahoma.

As we hit the runway, it felt like my heart dropped into my stomach. Once we came to a complete stop, all of the Marshalls got up and quickly exited the plane, except for one of them. All I could see from my window was the corner of a brick building. After seeing the women get up to get off the plane, we never saw them again. We were all staring out of the window wondering where they had went.

Once the Marshalls unloaded us from the plane, to our surprise, we were actually inside the institution. Our feet never touched the ground. I was astonished by it. Then we wobbled down a long hallway where a group of Marshalls were waiting for us to take the shackles off. As they removed the shackles from us, they placed us in a large holding tank. At that time we were all given information forms to fill out. After we completed the forms we went to see the Physician Assistant (PA) and the case workers.

The PA told me that I was healthy after checking my blood pressure and temperature and asking me a few questions. Then I went to see the case worker, Mr. Brown. He was a black man with a serious attitude. As I walked in the office he spoke up.

What are you in here for," he asked?

"For selling drugs," I replied.

"Are you affiliated with any gangs? Do you have any enemies? Did you assist the government? Do you want to go to general population?"

"I'm not affiliated with any gangs, nor am I afraid of anyone. I didn't assist the government and I want to go to general population," I answered.

I was assigned to a cellon the fifth floor. There I was given a bedroll and a cup with a short toothbrush and some government toothpaste and deodorant. Once I got to the fifth floor I was assigned to cell number 521, which Was a two man cell. Every floor had three TV Rooms, a large day room, with a kitchen and dining area. There were also four telephone booths. All of the calls that we made were collect. The only person that I could call was my mother, because she was the only person who's number that I knew which accepted collect calls. None of my children's mothers phones accepted collect calls. Shortly after I got into the cell, I was given a cellie named Smokey. he was a cool brother from East St. Louis, Illinois. Therefore, we were homeboys. Once we got ourselves situated, we chopped it up in conversation.

"Are you from Washington Park," I asked?

"Nope, I'm from Virginia Park, but I grew up on 33rd street," he said.

"What prison are you coming from, Smokey?"

"I'm coming from USP Florence Colorado. What about you," he asked?

"Oxford Wisconsin Medium. Oh my bad Smokey, I'm from Springfield, Illinois."

"I use to hang out in the John Hay Homes Project. You might know my people."

"What's their name," I asked?

"Hicks and Robinson. There's a gang of them there."

"I know who you are talking about, Marvin and Frank."

"Yeap, Black Marvin and big Frank are my cousins." About 2: 30 in the morning, the guard came to our cell and told Smokey to wrap 'em up and he would be back to get him in a few minutes. While waiting on the guard to come back to get Smokey, we exchanged contact information. We wrote it down on our property sheets.

"Where are you headed, Smokey?"

"FCI Greenville."

"You are going to the crib home front."

"It's a blessing man, I was out there in those Colorado mountains for five years. "Take care of yourself homie."

A couple of days later I got another cellie. He was an eighteen year old Puerto Rican guy named Ced. He spoke very fluent English. I could tell that he was scared to death. I immediately took a liking to him and took him under my wing. I educated Ced on how to do his time day by day and mind his own business. We also read the Holy Bible everyday and night and prayed. A week later, Ced left to go back to court to be sentenced. After being at the Oklahoma City Holding Institution for about seven weeks, a guard came by m cell saying . . .

"Joiner, wrap 'em up, you're out of here." While waiting for the guard to come back for me I said to myself that I was about to take my second plane ride. A few minutes later, he came back and took me downstairs to R&D. I looked at the clock and it was 1:30 a.m. in the morning. The guards placed about thirty of us in a holding tank, then gave us a brown bag. Inside of it was a bologna sandwich, milk, two boiled eggs and an apple.

At 3:30 a.m., after being dressed out and shackled we were escorted to the BOP bus. We arrived at FCI Yazoo City, Mississippi at 3:50 p.m. As we pulled up to the institution there were two white trucks that pulled up behind us and got out with their rifles. We had to remain on the bus until the four p.m. count cleared, which is the most important count in the federal system, because they have to call it in to Washington D.C. everyday. Once the count was clear, we were escorted into the Receiving Department. After the guard took the shackles off of us, we were given an orange jumpsuit with SHU on the back of them, which stood for Special Housing Unit. Afterwe got dressed, a case worker came and talked to us. I walked into Ms. Johnson's office and she asked me three questions.

"Do you have any enemies? Did you assist the government? Do you want to go to general population?"

"I don't have any enemies here. The only person that I know here is my brother. No, I did not assist the government. Yes, I would like to go to general population." After Ms. Johnson spoke with us, a guard came and took us all to the SHU. He told us that they didn't have bed space on the compound.

I wondered to myself why they even brought us there if they didn't have bed space for us. Well I must have actually been thinking out loud because the guard heard me.

"Young man," said the guard. "This is prison, not Princeton!" I took that as him saying that this was jail, not Yale. After being in the SHU for three days, I was released to the compound, which is general population. I was assigned to A-Unit.

My cellie was a guy named House from Atlanta. He was a down to earth brother who worked in unicor. Unicor is the prison's modern day slave factory.

The inmates who work in unicor make different equipment for other prisons, such as mail bags, cable, clothes, and furniture. They also make stuff for the government and military as well. Even though I m against working in unicor, because I know it's modern day slavery and cheap labor for the government, it's the best paying job in the federal system. Some guys make five hundred dollars per month. After House and I introduced ourselves to one another, he threw his PSR on the desk and asked me to check it out when I got time. As he was on his way out of the cube, I told him that I would have mine for him in a couple of days or as soon as I got my property.

Once I got situated I walked down to the commissary to purchase some snack food. While standing in the commissary line, my brother Cheek walked up behind me. I turned to see who it was, careful not to hit him. We gave each other a hug and thanked God that we were together again. Cheek introduced me to a few of the guys. Most of them was Christian brothers. A few minutes later, I heard the commissary guard calling my name. I asked Cheek would he like for me to get him anything.

"Nope, I'm good bro.," he replied. I decided to buy him a pint of banana pudding ice cream anyway He helped me carry my bag of goodies back to my unit, then he headed back to work.

A few days later, I got my property while House was at work, so I placed my PSR on his bed The reason that we wanted to show each other our paperwork is so that we would know that neither of us was a rat, snitch, or hot ass nigga. These terms identify people who assisted the government in the prosecution of another person. That evening when House got off work, he found my PSR on his bed. As I walked into our cubicle, House said, "L.J., you're 100%. L. J., one thing about living in cubicles, you really don't have any privacy. The guy who lives on the top bunk can see everything that you are doing. Oh yea, make sure that you sleep in the opposite direction from the guy beside you, so he want be looking, snoring, and breathing his stinking breath in your face."

After being at Yazoo City for almost a month, I was given an initial Team Meeting. An initial Team Meeting is when you meet with your unit team for the first time, which consist of a unit manager, case manager, and a counselor.

You must see them every six months until you have a year left to serve on your sentence I then you'll see them every three months. During this meeting, ymr unit team make recommendations for you about things that they want you to do.

As I walked into my unit team's office, they didn't speak to me nor did they invite me to have a seat, so I took it upon myself to take a seat.

"Listen," said my Case Manager. "You're going to do exactly what we tell you to do. You're going to get into GED programs, ACE classes, and the walking program. Do you understand that," she stated firmly?

"Are you done yet," I replied?

"Yes, and I'm waiting for you to let me know that you understand me," she said. Then I got up out of the chair and hit the table with them looking at me like I was going to just walk out, but I had something to say.

"Now you listen and the rest of you all in this room . . . I'm not going to do a damn thing that you just told me to do, and the best thing that y'all can do for me is to leave me alone. Let me do these twenty years the best way that I can." I proceeded to walk out of the office, slamming the door behind me.

Then next day while standing by the Chow Hall talking with a few guys from Mississippi, I heard my name announced over the loud speaker—"Joiner, 10642-026, report to R&D immediately." On my way to R&D, I said to myself that maybe the court gave me some action on my appeal like my attorney said they would.

Once I got to R&D and entered, I was greeted by a nice looking lady who looked very familiar to me. She asked me where I was from.

"Springfield, Illinois," I replied.

"I went to school with a guy that kind of looks like you. He sounds like you too, but he's from Cleveland, Mississippi," she stated.

"I know those Joiner's because I am one of them. Stop playing, I know right."

"No you're not one of them," she said.

"I went to Pearman, Margrett Green, and Cleveland High," I said.

"Well, now that we know each other, what have you done, because they're transferring you?"

"I haven't done anything. I've only been here for about a month," I said.

"You're getting an improper institution adjustment transfer to Mckean, Pennsylvania," she said after looking on the computer. We heard another guard coming in the door, so we stopped talking and pretended as if I was signing my property sheet. After the other guard went to the back, she decided to tell me her name. She put her finger over her mouth as if to say keep it to myself.

I actually couldn't believe it was her. She looked very sexy and fine. I had a look on my face like, dang I messed up, she might would've gave me some action if the time was right. As I got ready to walk out of the door, she took a quick peep to see where the guard was, then she walked up to me and said softly, "Whatever you are thinking, you just may be right." She winked her eye at me and smiled. I just smiled and shook my head like damn.

As I came out of R&D, Cheek was waiting to hear what they wanted with me. "So what did they want with you, bro.," asked Cheek?

"They are transferring me to Mckean, Pennsylvania for improper institution adjustment."

"L.J. I'm going to see who I can talk to to see what is really going on."

"Even though I'm going to miss you, I'm good. I really don't like this joint anyway."

"Bro. I hate to see you go, but I can respect what you are saying."

"Cheek, just as we were reunited back together here, we will meet up again. The next day I was given a bus ride to the Memphis Airport. Once again, I found myself waiting on the bus for the Feds 'Continental' plane. Once I got on the plane, we made three stops before landing at the airport in Harrisburg, Pennsylvania. I was then taken by BOP bus to the holding unit at Lewisburg. As we arrived at USP Lewisburg, it looked like a big red castle with a tall wall around it. Once we went through the R&D process, we were taken to the holdover unit. Just walking through the holdover court, it felt like death was in the air.

Once I got situated, I looked out of the window onto the compound and there were dogs, cats and friendly rabbits hanging out with the inmates. On the inside where we were, there were ants, roaches, rats, and cats that would jump in through the window and hang out with us. The only thing that was good about the big red castle is that they fed us good. After being there for a week, I was taken to my destination which was FCI Mckean. This insitution was known throughout the Federal Prison System as "Mckean the Dream." If an individual really wanted to change his life and help himself to be a better person or prepare for release, Mckean was the place to be. They had Culinary Arts, Personal Training, Dental Program, Barber Class, Janitorial, and Electrician Program. The certificates were provided by the Department of Labor and other known institutions. Many of the nearby colleges came to the prison and offered college courses that you could receive degrees in. In every housing unit, there were three pool tables, table tennis, foos ball, ping pong, and all kinds of board games. There were also four vending machines in the units. The telephones were always busy on Friday, Saturday, and Sunday because they stayed on until three a.m. The guys loved the phone hours, because they could keep up with their girlfriends . . . or at least they thought.

I was assigned to an eight man room. All of my cell mates were cool. We looked out for each other and we would make a meal for the room every weekend.

We all chipped in on paying this one brother that would clean our room Monday thru Friday. On the weekends everyone was responsible for cleaning their own area. After being at Mckean for a week, I was approached by a guy who lived in my unit. His name was Panama.

"Can I talk to you for a minute," he requested? There's something I must tell you. I got something hid in your mattress. I need you to ask all of your cellie's to step out for a couple of minutes after the four p.m. count clear."

"Okay, I will do that." During the four O' clock count I shared it with my roomates and told them to step out when they see him coming. Then I told them to rush back into the room. I saw Panama coming toward the room.

"Here he comes," I told my roommates. "Step out and then rush back in."

I must say, my cell mates carried the plan out to perfection. Just as Panama was raising the mattress up, all of my cell mates came rushing back into the room. Panama immediately dropped the mattress back down and attempted to leave the room. "Oh no! You need to get whatever you have in the mattress out right now," I said. "You really didn't think that I wasn't going to tell them, did you? You ·were putting all of us in harms way!.."

Then he walked slowly back over to my bed and lifted my mattress up.

About thirty seconds later he came out with a bag of prison knives, better known as shanks. After he showed us the knives, we told him that he owe us fifty bucks worth of commissary for eight weeks, because he had placed us all in a bad position. If the guard would have came into the room and found the knives, even though we had no knowledge that they were in the room, we all would've gone to SHU and been transferred to another institution.

About three days after the knives incident, I went to the education department to take an entry test so that I could get into the Culinary Arts Program. After being handed the test, the instructor told us that we could leave one we finished. I proceeded to take the test, and once I finished, I got up and went and handed it to my instructor, just as I had seen other inmates that had finished before me. After he got finished with his pat search on me

I asked him, "Sir, I would like to know why you patted me down, and nobody else?"

"First of all, this is my classroom, but since you must know, you looked like you were cheating," he replied.

"Well sir, I think you owe me an apology for embarrassing me in front ot the class since you didn't find any cheat notes on me." His face turned red as fire.

"I don't owe no inmate nothing." Sir, what's your name," I asked?

"Why? I'm not gong to lose my job if you write me up," he said.

"It's not a matter of whether you lose your job or not, it's about you being professional." I left the education department and went to speak with my counselor concerning the issue.

"He should have apologized to you, but some people think it takes their authority away if they admit that they were wrong," said my counselor.

"Mr. B's, I can read between the lines. Thank you."

The next day in class, Mr. Straham gave each on of us our test score out loud. He then came around to show us our score and the questions that we missed. As he got around to me I spoke up.

"I don't want to see mine Sir I'm good with the 3.7 that you said I made." Then he put it in my face. "Mr. Straham, I told you that I didn't want to see my score."

"It's not what you want to do, it's what I want you to do," he said.

"You got five seconds to get this paper out of my face." Suddenly, I knocked the paper out of my face and tried to get up, but he pushed me back down in the desk. Then he told me to get up and get out his class. I heard my buddy, Kelli tell me something.

"L.J., don't do it man," said Kelli. As I got up out of my desk to leave the classroom, I took two steps and turned around and caught Mr. Straham with a haymaker right hand! Blood just shot out of the top of his left eye. Once he fell to the floor, I kicked him a couple of times. The female teacher across the hall hit her dueces and kept yelling for me to stop it. I went ahead and got against the wall, because I knew the goon-squad was coming for me, and I didn't want to give them another reason to beat the crap out of me.

As all of the guards came through the door, Mr. Straham started screaming and pointing at me.

"He assaulted me! He assaulted me," he shouted with blood allover his face! The first three guards that came rushing in the door, came over to me and told me to turn around and cuff up.

"I'm not gong to cuff up out here," I told them. Just as I said that, the lieutenant came through the door. One of the three guards told him that I had refused to cuff up.

"That's his right," said the lieutenant. "Walk him outside." Once I got outside, I turned around and allowed one of the guards to handcuff me. My reason for refusing to cuff up was, you never let the guards handcuff you around other inmates, because someone that you might have a beef with, just might decided to take advantage of the opportunity while you're defenseless.

Once I got to the SHU I was placed in the holding cell until the lieutenant came to the holding cell with a guard to get me. Then I was taken into the Lieutenant's Office. It was a small room in the SHU. He read me the incident report. "You're being charged with violence, assault on a government employee. If proven, you can and will be charged in a federal court and prosecuted. "L. T., I plead not guilty to this charge under policy statement 3420-09," I said. In short term, P. S. 3420-09 in the BOP policy that govern the conduct of the BOP staff in which action to assault Mr. Straham was provoking by him in which P. S. 3420-09 prohibits. During my conversation with the lieutenant, I told him that I wanted to call my classmates as witnesses on my behalf. Before the Lieutenant could ask me the next question, a guard came through the door with a handful of copout forms from my classmates telling what happened between Mr. Straham and I. After looking at a few of the copouts, the Lieutenant looked at me.

"Joiner, I must put you in the SHU until the issue is settled, for safety reasons." After the investigation, Mr. Straham was suspended and I was transferred to a lower security institution in Waseca, Minnesota. This is the place where I decided to get off of the prison merry-go-round and seek a sense of direction for my future and continue to fulfill my professional cooking dream.

CHAPTER 14

A SENSE OF DIRECTION

While out in the free world as we call it in prison, I had no sense of direction, purpose or meaning to my life. I didn't value anything. It was all about me. I simply took life for granted. I was so blind that I couldn't even see that all of my 'so called' friends were only hanging around me because of what I had and what I was doing for them. If you would've put my brain in a bat's head at this time . . . the bat would've flew backwards! I really didn't love anybody, not even myself, because when you love somebody, you never place them in harms way nor do you leave them when they really need you the most.

I am a firm believer that the way that an individual see life, that's the way that individual shapes and lives their life. I decided to live a lifestyle that I truly thought was exciting and fruitful at the same time but in return, I got a two hundred and thirty-five month sentence in federal prison for a conspiracy to distribute crack cocaine. I will make it very simple and real clear that nobody put a gun to my head to force me to sell drugs. I simply made the choice myself. As crazy as this may sound, going to prison saved my life and saved me from my worst enemy . . . myself. It also gave me a new outlook on life over a period of time.

My sense of direction started at Petersburg Illinois County Jail. I began to seek God with my whole heart, because I knew that if anybody could help me, it would be Him. I prayed and read my bible everyday and night. I remember reading the eleventh chapter of the book of Mark, verse twenty-two which said'

"And Jesus answered saying to them, Have faith in God." I also read chapter one of the book of Luke, verse thirty-seven which said, "For with God nothing will be impossible." I know what you might be thinking. Because I was in jail and headed to prison, I wanted to be religious. Well, I knew God at an early age because it was a household rule for us to go to church on Sunday.

Therefore, I at least knew to call on Him. I guess I forgot about Him when I moved to Illinois and started selling drugs. God has a way of getting our attention, conscience of it or not. Many people believe that prison is a setup to entrap the black man and woman. That might be somewhat true and poverty and drugs may be two of the main reason's that we fall into the trap, but nevertheless, the choice is still up to us. I am also a firm believer that we as people allows poverty to become a controlling state of mind due to history, lack of education, laziness and most of all, our pride. We are quick to say "I'm not working at McDonald's. On the other hand, if we swallow our pride, change our attitude and state of mind, maybe we can own our own McDonald's instead of working at one. The only somebody that can put a limit on you is you. I once heard a man say, Whatever the mind of a man can believe and conceive, the mind of a man can achieve it." Therefore, always believe in yourself. I must admit in the beginning of my prison sentence before reality kicked in, I blamed everyone but L.J., myself. I kept justifying my actions and bad choices to myself by saying, "You're not a bad guy and you helped a lot of people." I was very angry and mad with the world and because I was hurting, I hurt other people, not physically, but mentally with words.

One day while walking the prison yard at FCI Oxford, an old man called me and said, "L.J., you got a minute, I would like to talk to you."

"Sure Old Man Zack, what's on your mind," I replied?

As we began to stroll the track together he said, "Listen L.J.! You don't have to walk around with an attitude. You need to focus on doing your time and not let this time do you. Work on your case."

"Old Man Zack, I appreciate your advice, but you don't know me like that sir. "You're right, L. J., I don't know you like that, but I see something in you underneath your toughness. I see greatness in you, but you must first swallow your pride. I promise you that if you do so, you won't choke to death," he told me. I could only laugh, because it was so profound and it was also my first time hearing the phrase. Old Man Zack's phrase—"Swallow your pride, you won't choke to death" was the first seed of change planted in my life. A week after talking with Old Man Zack, I enrolled in a class called PMA, which is the acronym for Positive Mental Attitude. The PMA course supported everything that Old Man Zack shared with me. Even though our conversation had sparked the fire of change, the choice or decision to change was still up to me. No one changes unless they want to. One of the biggest fears known to man is to change! We as people hate to change, because it requires us to step outside of our comfort zone into the unknown which we fear. We also worry about what people are going to say if we change even though it's for our own good. We worry if we'll still fit in with the guys.

I want you to know that I am part of this persuasion, "if an individual say that they are your friend, and don't respect that you want to make a positive change in your life, he or she is not your friend. A real friend will always have your best interest at heart. Since I didn't have a high school diploma, I enrolled in the GED program in order to receive my General Equivalency Diploma. It's mandatory in the federal prison system to enroll in the GED program if you don't have a high school diploma or verified GED.

If you refused to enroll in the GED program, you would lose twelve days of good time per year. Once I received my GED, I felt the burden of failure lifted off of me and the doors of opportunity began to open. I couldn' t wait to send my children a copy of my GED diploma. I was now in a better position to challenge them to get their education. Our children doesn't always do as we say, but they mostly do as we do, whether positive or negative. After receiving my GED, I began to take several college and apprenticeship courses to pass my time and prepare for the future. I decided to take a Hotel and Restaurant Management course to learn how to run a profitable and effective business. I can truly say that those courses and the completion of them renewed my hope and gave me self gratification. I began to focus on self development, self worth, and not the selfishness of self fulfillment.

What is self worth? Self worth is the sense of one's own value or worth as a person; self esteem; self respect. Your self worth is built on the choices that you make to become the best you that you can be in life It takes self denial and hard work to become a 'good you especially in today's society that we live in. We live in a crab's society where whenever you try to move up in life, someone is always trying to pull you back down or trying to keep you down because of envy and jealousy. There are haters all around us, family members, associates and even our so called best friends As crazy as it may sound, people will hate you for trying to be a better you. Self worth is a forever learning process because there is always room for self improvement in life. We must learn to love and value ourselves more than anybody else and stop killing ourselves and our dreams. I now understand the importance of making your own decisions and not allowing yourself to be driven by other people's opinion of you, because they really don't know you, your self worth, your potential, or the hero that lives in you. Once you understand your true self worth, you can use the wisdom, knowledge, and understanding to pursue your goals, dreams, purpose, and ambitions and help others to do the same. I thought my self worth was based on my money, cars, and the reputation of my street image. Your self worth has nothing to do with your money, cars, image, nor how much you know or thing you know, it only focuses on self. You must make a commitment to yourself and believe in yourself and know that you can make something out of your life in spite of your past mistakes. You must also know in your heart that you have the power within you to overcome any obstacles that stand in your way. In order to live a peaceful and fruitful life takes boldness, courage, patience, ambition initiative, and a lot of self discipline. With a sense of direction, knowledge, wisdom and understanding, I now know that my imprisonment was meant by the enemy to destroy me, my hopes and dreams but it turned out to be a blessing. I can honestly say that without my imprisonment, I would not be the man that I am today, but thanks be unto God, because it's only by His grace and mercy that I am who I am. But on the other hand, if it wasn't for my mess, you wouldn't be reading my life story.

I grew up understanding an old popular saying, "All that don't kill you, will make you stronger." I believe that everything happens for a reason and serves a purpose in life. My imprisonment opened my eyes to many different things and taught me one of the greatest gifts in life which is love. I learned how to love myself and others in prison. I also learned that it's okay for a man to cry and it's okay to swallow your pride. As the old hymm says, I was once lost, but now I'm found. I was once blind but now I see. I can now say that a set back in life can be a blessing for you and give you an opportunity to get re-focussed and get back on the right track in life with a fresh sense of direction~ a purpose, and add new meaning to your life Once again, prison saved my life and saved me from my worst enemy being myself.

It gave me an opportunity to find myself and leave my own prison. It's not the razor wire, bars, or fences that make a prison, but it's simply the state of mind. I thank God for bringing me up out of the pit of hell out of the mirey clay, and setting my feet upon a rock and establishing m; solid foundation Since I now have a sense of direction, I understand that I can't change the past, but I can do some thing about the present and look to the future.

My message to you is that your past is never done with you until you are done with it. Your greatest success and achievement in your life lies ahead of you. You are more creative than you can imagine, and far more intelligent than you think. The happiest moments in your life is right around the corner.

Therefore, stay focussed, believe in yourself and never give up on your dreams, visions, or plans. The only individual that can place a limit on you is you. It was through my imprisonment, and all of the pain and suffering that I found a sense of direction for my life. It's where I realized my purpose.

I also discovered a lot of hidden talents and skills that I didn't even know that I possessed. I have the ability to write amazing stage plays and skits.

I learned how to fight the court system in search of justice according to the law. Every individual who don't have a sense of direction for their life only place themselves in harms way.

CHAPTER 15

COOKING IN PRISON

As a young boy I dreamed of being a professional cook/chef, but I never thought that my dream would come to pass while serving time in federal prison.

After being processed through R&D, I was assigned to C-Unit. On my way up the stairs to the unit, I met my homeboy, Tyson whom I hadn't seen since the Feds got him in 1992. He was coming down the stairs. As we made eye contact, he shouted to me.

"My nigga, L.J., better known as Woo Daddy. I got me a real chef here with me now." He walked me on up the stairs and showed me my cell. Once I threw my bedroll on the bunk, we engaged in a man hug and shook hands. "L. J., let me walk down to the commissary so I can hook you up with a few things until you get your property."

"I'm good man, I got money on my books," I replied. "But take my shopping list and order whatever we need to make a few meals"

"I see you haven't changed You're the same guy that you were on the bricks . . . you just have a sense of direction to your life now he told me.

We chat for a minute about what we liked to eat and cook. I ordered ten bags of pre-cooked rice, three cheese rice, four pouches of chili with beans, soy sauce, squeeze cheese, five turkey logs, two chocolate chip cookies, two bags of Doritoe Chips, a bag of onion, and a bag of green pepper. I also ordered:" case of Ramen Vegetable Soup. I almost forgot to purchase a few picture tickets so I could take some pictures with my family in the visiting room.

Tyson also purchased pretty much the same items that I did except he ordered Mackerel and Tuna Fish.

As we got back to the unit and got situated Tyson introduced me to all of the guys in the unit. He was very popular in the unit and on the compound.

My cell mate was a guy named Veron. He was a smooth brother with a mean B' s game. Veron was from Baltimore, Maryland. Tyson and him were very tight with each other. The next day Tyson took me to the kitchen where he worked He introduced me to the food service administrator. What's up Jack In The Box," said Tyson as we walked into the office. "Those 49ers don't look so hot."

"What do you want to bet? Make it light on yourself. I bet you twenty push ups in the middle of the chow hall."

"Bet" said Jack In The Box!

"Jack In The Box, I got you a real cook but you must take care of him."

"Do you know how many of these guys on both shifts said the same thing," he replied kind of sarcastically?

"You're right but my homeboy can show you better than I can tell you said Tyson.

"Okay, I'm going to put him on the P.M. shift with you." As we walked out of the door, I saw one of the A.M. cooks from Oxford, Wisconsin.

"What's up L. J., man we need a good cook on A.M.," he said.

"Guess what homie, they just hired me on the P.M. shift Gus."

"We are going to keep L. J. on the P.M. shift," said Tyson. A week later I was assigned to the food service P.M. cook shift.

My first day on the P.M. cook shift, I was asked what are the ingredients for Beef Stroganoff. I told them that I need beef strips or beef cube shortening, flour, pepper, salt, beef base, vinegar, tomato puree, mushrooms, sour cream, bay leaves, and onions and brown sugar.

I can live with that replied the supervisor. "So what do you need to make chicken Ala king?"

I began to rattle off what was needed. "Chicken diced or chunks, mushrooms, green pepper, pimentos, milk, chicken base, cooking wine, shortening, and white pepper. You can either serve it over rice or noodles," I said.

"My name is Joe," said the supervisor. Joiner, you just might know what you're doing. After being in the kitchen for about a week and doing my thing, guys in the kitchen started hating on me, but on the other hand, the guards was praising me and my work. A couple of weeks later I transferred to the A.M. cook shift. As I walked into the kitchen at 4:45 a.m., I was greeted by my homie, Gus.

"L.J., I appreciate you coming over here to help me,"

"So you helped pull this move, huh?" Gus just fell out laughing. "Homie, 4:00 o'clock came so fast. I felt like I had just laid down when the guard tapped my bed."

"L.J., let me give you the 411 on how things work on this shift. It's this hot ass dude named Marvin that think he runs the cook shift and the whole kitchen. The guards give him the green light, but I let him know that he can't dictate how much of this government food I can take. I get my hustle on. This is how I survive in here!."

"Gus let's go in the kitchen and help the guys out," I suggested.

"They really don't have nothing but cold cereal and doughnuts. After breakfast is over we will start on the lunch. I want you to make that BBQ sauce that you use to make in Oxford."

"So what all do we have with the BBQ chicken," I asked?

"We have greens, cornbread, yams, mac & cheese, and we must fry about fifty pieces of chicken for the staff dining room and a hundred pieces for us five cooks." Once breakfast was over I told Gus that I would make the BBQ sauce and the cheese sauce for the mac & cheese. I would enter any BBQ taste test competition with this recipe. This Barbecue Sauce is the bomb.

2 #10 cans catsup
1 cup liquid smoke
1/2 quart white horseradish
4 medium onion, finely chopped
1/2 cup mustard
16 garlic cloves minced
3 fresh lemons, cut in cubes
4 cups brown sugar
1/2 cup worcestershir
1/2 cup chili powder
3/4 cup cayenne pepper

Place catsup and liquid smoke in a large pot, mix well, over medium heat.

Add white horseradish and next four ingredients and cook for ten to fifteen minutes, or until it begins to boil.

Stir in brown sugar and remaining ingredients. Let ingredients continue to cook for five minutes. Reduce heat to low, and simmer for about fifteen minutes.

Remove sauce from heat. Pour mixture through wire-mesh strainer into another pot or bowl, discarding solids. Now you have L. J. s Unique Barbecue Sauce in your home!

Once the food was cooked and lunch was started, the inmates rushed into the chow hall like mad Russians. All of the homies were walking around the Chow Hall saying, "My homies, Gus and L. J. did their thang with this meal."

Even though Gus helped prepare the meal, I got all of the credit, but I told them that Gus deserved the credit because he showed me how to do everything, which was a lie.

The next day, the Food Service Administrator called me into his office and asked me, "Joiner would you like to work in the staff kitchen?"

"With all do respect, no sir. I would like to get my feet a little more wet and work on my attitude."

Well, whenever you're ready just let me know," he said.

"Yes sir. Thank you." I really didn't want to work in the staff kitchen because you have to tap dance and put on the good inmate persona. You must always say yes sir or yes ma'am, or no sir no ma'am. There's a saying that states . . . "Everything is not for everybody" Working in the staff dining or kitchen wasn t for me. After proving myself day by day on the cook shift I was moved up to the grade two cook position, which meant I made thirty-one cents per hour, instead of twenty-three cents. Some of the guys started hating on me because of my cooking skills and the guards were praising me for my work, but they never expressed it to me or the homies. I must say, even though there was a little jealousy and intense at times between us cooks, it didn't add up to the danger and all of the bull jive that I went through while I was a line server. Twelve hundred hungry jokers came through the line three times a day to get their issue. Guys would come through the line mean mugging you trying to intimidate you. You have to be strong and stand your ground. It's not about whether you win the fight or not, what matters most in prison is that you make them realize that you will fight if it comes down to it. Fights broke out in the Chow Hall sometimes just because someone broke in line, reached over another guy's tray, or because the line server gave gave some fool a small piece of chicken or a small portion of lasagna. It would be a shame to call home and tell your family that you got killed over a piece of fried chicken or someone busted your head over a so called 'yard pimp'. Gus and I became business partners, hustling well together. We only sold cooked and raw meat. Now there was a serious penalty for being caught with raw meat, because you can't properly store it and therefore salmonella and other bacteria could contaminate the meat and cause food poisoning.

On chicken and hamburger days, we would have a line of customers outside of my unit like we were selling crack. We would even give some of the meat on consignment just like I did in the dope game. We would get paid in stamps or commissary. Just like the free world, we sometimes had problems with guys paying us. The white guys, Jews, Asians, Native Americans, Spanish guys, and Italians did not play with our money. Most of the white guys and Italians would have you to give them your name and prison ID number, and they would have money sent to our books every month. We would also sell them steaks and shrimp. A steak sold for a book of stamps or six dollars. A ten pound bag of shrimp sold for thirty dollars.

Every Saturday and Sunday we had to prepare brunch. We would have sausage, pancakes, syrup, oatmeal with cinnamon, hash browns, leftover pastries from coffee hour and eggs to order. My guy, Gus and I would jump on the two grills and bang the eggs to order out. Most of the white guys wanted their eggs over-easy or sunny side up. Asians wanted theirs cooked medium.

Latinos took whatever you gave them, and the black guys wanted theirs hard fried or scrambled.

As Ramadan came around for the Muslim guys, just as the Christian Community grew when they had their feast, so did the Muslim Community during Ramadan. They would fast for thirty days from sun up until sunset each day.

Brothers who you had no idea was Muslim would all of a sudden be saying, "As-Salaam-Alaikum" to one another.

During Ramadan, I was responsible for making sure that we put food to the side for them all thirty days. They would have the entire dining room to themselves. One day during Ramadan, my guy, D.J. walked up to the homie, Pete saying, "If you wanna get big, you better eat the pig."

"Nigga don't you see me with my kufi on, I don't want to talk about no damn pork," said Pete. As time passed, I became the head cook on the A.M. shift. Gus was relocated to the butcher shop. The hustling business went to a whole different level. Since I was now the head cook I got first bid on fruits and vegetables, as well as pastries. The same way I took care of my workers in the dope game, I looked out for my assistant cooks. I never tried to police the government's food, but my motto was "Don't take from the meal.

If you need something, just let me know and I will get it for you." My reason for this motto was because everyone is not blessed with financial assistance from the outside world, so I made sure that they got their issue.

Every meal that I made, I put love into my work. I would check all of the products before they were served. In other words, I never sent a dish out that I wouldn't eat myself. Even in prison holidays are special times of the year, especially Thanksgiving and Christmas. The Bureau of Prisons even have a heart at Christmas time. They give every inmate a nice size bag filled with chocolate, cookies, candies, and chips. They also place special items from the commissary shopping list such as strawberry doughnuts, turtle candy, caramel popcorn, graham crackers, chili fritos, pound cake, clams, and smoked oysters in the bags. Holidays are also a sad and depressed time.

After seeing a few guys hang themselves over there women leaving them through Dear John Letters, and especially during the Christmas Holidays, I decided to join the inmate companionship watch.

Whenever an inmate became very depressed and seemingly hopeless, he was placed on suicide watch, so that he couldn't hurt himself or anybody else.

They were put in a room, naked. During my shift on suicide watch I would always think about when I first came to prison. I would basically try to put myself in their shoes. I would stand at the door and talk with them for hours.

This would consist of mostly allowing them to do the talking and I would just encouragement. "Everything will be alright. Your family needs you and they love you. You also have other people who care about you. You have to stay strong."

I always said this to them.

One Saturday while preparing brunch, I got burned by the steam. While stirring the oatmeal, one of the cook's helpers opened the pot that was beside me with strawberry syrup in it and the steam got me on the back of my right forearm. I immediately went and reported the accident to my supervisor just in case a body check was called due to a fight. Remember, a body check is called when there has been a fight and the guards are trying to figure out who was involved.

That same day that I got burned, my queens came to visit me. As I was leaving medical, I heard my name called for visit. "Joiner, you have a visit.

Report to the visitation room." As I entered the visiting room with my right arm wrapped up, I felt all eyes on me. I could only imagine what everyone was thinking, especially my family. Once I made it over to the area where my family was seated, they gave me the twenty one question test: What happened?

Did somebody stab you? Did somebody cut you? Did somebody hurt your arm?"

"None of the above," I answered. "One of the cooks accidentally opened the pot next to me. "I'm good. It's all part of being a cook." I pulled put my medical papers and showed it to them. I could tell that it helped to put them at ease, not that they thought I was lying, they was just concerned.

About a year after I became the head cook, my unit team told me that the institution in Coleman, Florida were offering the Culinary Arts Program. They asked me if I was interested in it. I told them that I don't know and that it was kind of far away from my family. I told them that I had to discuss it with my family and get back with them. I did thank them for considering me.

The next day at work, I shared it with my supervisor in the kitchen.

"Joiner, you got what it takes to be a chef," he told me. "You got knowledge, you learn quickly and you have good people skills, as well as leadership skills."

"Thank you, Slick Rick," I replied. A couple of days later Rick gave me a letter of recommendation, which was signed by the food service administrator. He told me to give my unit team a copy of the letter It read, Since inmate Joiner has been assignment to Food Service, he has been an asset to the department. He has been assigned to the A.M. cook shift performing various tasks such as: cooking meats, pastas, vegetables, starches, soups, gravies, and assorted grill items.

Inmate Joiner is very prompt and dependable. He always conducts himself as a gentleman and gets along with inmates and staff alike. I would recommend inmate Joiner to any school or food service department.

In 2002, I decided to take a Catering and Gourmet Cooking Course to enhance my skills and knowledge, as well as to receive some type of diploma or certificate. In February of 2003, I completed the Catering and Gourmet Cooking Course. After receiving the diploma I began to refocus on my childhood dream of being a professional cook. I began to spend more time studying cook books and recipes, and thinking about my future outside of prison. One day I walked into the barbershop and one of the barbers asked me to read an article about a brother who found his calling as a cook while behind bars. Someone else showed me the same article in a USA Today Newspaper.

There were these two old men, one was black and the other one was white.

They would sit in front of the unit and talk about how they started their business. Both of their names was Mr. Johnson. We would call them Johnson and Johnson foundation, because if you wanted to develop a plan and a foundation for your life when you are released, they were the ones to talk to. One day as I was walking out of the unit, Johnson and Johnson asked me, could they talk to me for a minute L.J.?"

"Sure, what's on y'all mind sir," I said.

"We've been watching you for a while. You are very respectful and very smart, but we notice that you seem to be somewhat unstable and undecided about what you really want in life. We would like to thank you for caring about us in the kitchen as a whole. A good and decent cooked meal in prison does a man well."

Then the White Mr. Johnson said, "I see you having your own restaurant when you get out. I would like to talk with you at least three times a week."

"You got that," I replied. As I was walking off they both said . . .

"L.J.?, a man who fails to plan, he plan to fail, but a mind that is elevated to new heights never goes back to its origins1 mind-set,"

My daily talks with Johnson and Johnson began to rekindle the cooking fire that was within me, so I began to speak positive things in my own life.

I began to think outside of the prison walls. I began spending more time in the law library, taking cooking courses, and writing plays and skits. My homies began to ask stupid questions. "What' s up L. J.? I know this time is not getting to you? Are you stressing over you and Jody girl?"

"Check this out out fellas, it's none of the above, I'm just trying to think outside of the box and trying to fight my case. There has to be a loop hole in my case. But on the other hand we can still get together and make us a feast on the weekend."

"Well tomorrow is Friday and they're having spaghetti in the kitchen, so what's up with some chef L.J, fried rice said El Dog.

"I'm going to use this recipe when I get out. I would put this recipe to work in any fried rice cook off contest.

L.J., you ain't like that for real,'! said Tex.

You don't have to pump me up brother man, I'm going to do it. But just for the record ability"

I'm not cocky, but I am very confident in my God given This is what we need guys for the four of us:

2 7oz. bags pre—cooked white rice
2 7oz. bags cheese rice
2 California Vegetable Cup Ramen Noodles
2 tablespoons garlic powder
2 tablespoons soy sauce
4 tablespoons olive oil
4 cups of water
3 medium onion, finley chopped
2 large green bell peppers
Add meat of choice if you desire

Now let me show you guys how to make L.J. Microwave Unique Fried Rice:

Place white rice and cheese rice in a large plastic microwave bowl mix well.

Add next four ingredients to the rice, stir well.

Set microwave on twenty minutes, place bowl into microwave and let ingredients cook for 3 minutes. Take rice out and stir well with a butter knife_ Repeat this step again. Take rice out, add one cup of water, stir well, cook for 3 minute. Repeat this step again. Add onion and bell pepper to the rice, stir well, add cup of water, place rice back in the microwave. Cook for 3 minutes.

Add 1/2 cup of water cook for 3 minutes. Repeat this step again, but only use the two minutes that remain.

Now you guys know how to make L.J.'s Microwave Unique Fried Rice Therefore, I won't be making it for you guys anymore.

"Man! I got to get my priorities in order. I can't go back to the free world with my same state of mind that I had when I came in here. I got a half dozen children out there who need me, as well as other youth who look up to me as a role model. I must see this minor setback as an opprtunity to get myself together so I can move ahead when I am released in life with a purpose.

I'll have a true sense of direction. I can do all things in Christ who strengthens me. I am going to pray the Serenity Prayer every day from now on:

God grant me the serenity to accept the things I cannot change, courage to change the things I can, and the wisdom to know the difference. Amen. I can't wait until I am released, so I can go home and cater our family reunion, my wedding, and bless others with my unique skills that flourished while serving time in prison. If I can make people smile in here with my cooking skills, I am ready to do the same in the free world.

CHAPTER 16

FIGHTING THE COURT SYSTEM

I use to believe what a person didn't know, it wouldn't hurt them. After being indicted by the federal government, I now know that saying is not true!

Because if I would've known half of what I know now about the federal government and the court system, my attorney would not have been able to help~he court to railroad me. I am serving a 235 month sentence on a ninety seven percent ghost dope conspiracy Ghost dope is and amount of drugs that the court hold you accountable for based on two witness statements for the government without any physical evidence and no drugs. Yes that's right, believe it or not, you don't have to get caught with the drugs in your possession~ nor do you have to sell it to an undercover cop or informant. They just need two government witnesses to say somewhat the same thing.

A conspiracy is an agreement between two or more people to commit a crime against the United States Government, knowingly. It is so easy to catch a conspiracy charge without having real knowledge of it. For example, say you let me use your cell phone and I call a drug dealer who is being investigated by the feds and I make arrangements to buy some drugs from him and I then give you your phone back and leave. Keep in mind that you don't know who I called nor did you hear the conversation. After I leave, he then called your cellphone and ask you have I left to come and get the package. Without thinking you say, "He's on his way now." You can very well be a part of a conspiracy that you have no real knowledge of.

There's several men and women who are serving a mandatory minimum sentence of 120 months in federal prison based on the above example that I gave. A mandatory minimum sentence is a sentence that the court must impose even though your sentence range may be lower. For example, you are charged with fifty grams or more of crack, the court must sentence you to

120 months, which is 10 years, because of the mandatory minimum, unless you cooperate with the government or get some type of departure in your sentence. There's a huge difference between the state court system and the federal court system. In the state court, you can buy your way out of a case if your money is right, or if you know the right people. As for the federal court, it don't matter how much money you have or who you know, because you are money and an investment as well as job security for the Federal Government and its staff.

Therefore, if the Federal Government can prosecute you, they are going to do so. There are judges, crooked cops, state officials, professional football and basketball players, as well as millionaires, blind people, crackheads, cripple, and crazy people in the federal system.

Most of us drug dealers, prior to our incarceration have no idea how the federal court system work. Since we are green and naive on how the system works, and don't have the money to hire a lawyer, the court appoints us one of their attorneys to represent us, who do very little work on our case, if any. Once the court appointed attorney comes and visit you, the first thing that comes out of his/her mouth is, "It don't look good for you, but the government is willing to make you a deal if you accept the plea agreement."

Now, without fully explaining the plea agreement to you, the court appointed attorney induces you into signing the plea agreement by threatening you with the phrase, "If you go to trial, you'll be found guilty, because you are going to have an all white jury who has never seen crack before, or they say they haven't. And if you're found guilty of fifty grams or more of crack, you can get a life sentence."

In 1999, the Seventh District denied my direct appeal. My court appointed attorney sent me a letter stating . . . "I am sorry but the Seventh Circuit denied your appeal and I don't see any issues to appeal to the Supreme Court."

After getting over the shock, I wrote my attorney a letter based on the appeal court reason for denying my appeal and asked her to sign an affidavit on my behalf admitting that she was ineffective in my case. A few weeks later I heard back from her.

"Joiner, 10642-026, you got legal mail," said the guard. As I made it back to my cell with the mail, I saw that it was my attorney responding to my letter.

It read, "As to the affidavit you want me to sign, I will think about it. No attorney, of course, likes to admit that he or she was incompetent, but I don't feel like I was incompetent in your case. I simply think that Ausa lied to me. I guess I was impressed with the big diploma he had on his office wall, indicating that he had graduated from Brigham Young University Law School. I thought Mormons were supposed to be religious and honest. Big surprise.

In turn, I wrote her a letter . . . "If you think the prosecute lied to you, that means you lied to me. I pray that you will find it in your heart to uphold justice by signing the affidavit for me," I said. After writing the letter to my attorney I said to myself that I couldn't believe that she had the nerve to tell me that she was impressed by a darn diploma hanging on the prosecutor's wall, who gave me twenty years. I must keep it real with you, I could care less about his diploma and him being a Mormon. They lie just like anybody else with a split in their mouth.

About a month later, I received a signed sworn affidavit form my attorney admitting to rendering ineffective assistance of counsel in my case. I began to tell myself, "I'm about to go home, I'm out of here." The next day I decided to share the good news with my homies.

"Remember when I told y'all that I sent a letter to my attorney asking her to sign an affidavit for me admitting to being ineffective. Guess what?"

"Don't lie man. Ain't no attorney going to admit to being ineffective, because they can be disbarred, sued and their reputation will be shot," Tex said. I reached into my pocket.

"Look fool! I'm not playing. I'm out of here for real just as soon as they give me a court date. "Boy, you're on your way out the door, said Doc P. "Please don't forget us when you hit the bricks."

"Hey guys, let's do a big boy nacho this weekend for L.J.," said Decatur.

"Congratulation" said Tex.

Since I had te affidavit from my attorney, I filed a pro-se 2255 motion claiming ineffective assistance of counsel. A pro-se motion is a motion that an inmate file to the court on his own instead of using an attorney. The court review the pro-se motion from a different point of view versus a motion prepared by a professional attorney.

While waiting on the court to rule on my 2255 motion, I got a letter from my attorney saying, "Please don't worry about Mr. Prosecute because I'm certainly not worried about him. I was just a little embarrassed about my letter being published to the court, but I'm past that. If the letter helps you, then it's worth any embarrassment I might have. If your 2255 goes anywhere, I will be happy to testify if you want me to."

Three months later, even though my ineffective assistance of counsel claim was supported with an affidavit from my attorney admitting to being ineffective and a letter from the attorney willing to testify on my behalf, the court denied my 2255 motion without an evidentiary hearing. In denying my 2255 motion, Judge Mills said, "The court is not persuaded by Ms. Deir's affidavit in which she admitted to being ineffective or incompetent." I must say that it almost took my breath when I turned to the last page of the court order and seen DENIED.

"This must be a mistake! There's no way that the court could have denied my motion with an affidavit from my attorney saying that she was ineffective,"

I said. I just lie on my bed all that day in disappointment.

The next day I had to face all of the homies who thought I was playing when I told them the court denied my motion. "L.J., stop playing man, when is your court date," said Tex.

"Look guys, I'm not playing. They denied me for real," I said.

That's crazy man. Those people are going to burn in hell for all of the wrong they are doing to us LJ" said Doc P.

"All I can say guys, "God must got something that He needs me to do in here." After my 2255 was denied, I filed a notice of appeal. The District Court then sent my notice of appeal to the Seventh Circuit, who then construed it to a request for a Certificate of Appealability.

On January 25, 2002, the Seventh Circuit Court of Appeals denied my request for a COA. In the response, the Seventh Circuit Appeals Court stated, "We find no substantial showing of the denial of a constitutional right."

Now there I was sitting there wondering how can the Court of Appeals say there was no substantial showing of the denial of a constitutional right when it is undisputed that my fifth and sixth amendment rights of the constitution was violated. In the same order, the court said, "We note that the District Court erred in stating that the statutory maximum for Joiner's offense is life imprisonment, the statutory maximum is actually 20 years. Nevertheless, because his sentence of 235 months is less than 20 years." I couldn't believe that the Appeals Court denied my COA even after it was noted that the court gave me incorrect information regarding my correct statutory maximum for my particular charge. I filed several motions afterward in search of justice . . . if it is a such thing as justice.

Every year in the federal system, around June we are given some type of hope that a law may change that will reduce our sentences. In 2007, the Sentencing Commission decided to give certain crack offenders a two level reduction in their sentences based on the disparity between crack cocaine and powder cocaine. There were several criteria that disqualified certain offenders. If a crack offender had a mandatory minimum sentence, a special plea sentence, a career offender, or it they were accountable for more than 4.5 kilograms of crack, he or she was ineligible.

All of us who were sentenced before 2007 had to wait until March 2008 to file for the two level reduction in our sentence. The court denied me a two level reduction in my sentence, because they said that even though I was found accountable for 1. 5 kilograms of crack at sentencing, I was still responsible for an excess of 4.5 kilograms. Once the court denied me the two level reduction, I decided to hire an investigative team and a school of law to research my case. While the research was being done on my case, a newsletter came out that alerted me to the fact that fraud had and is being committed in the district courts of Illinois, as well as the seventh circuit court of appeals. At the conclusion of the investigation and the research of my case, I was told that I received ineffective assistance of counsel, due process violation, prosecution misconduct, and judicial misconduct, as well as court fraud.

I would encourage anyone who is in prison to continue to educate yourself in the law especially concerning your charge and case as a whole. You just might find an error that will entitle you to a new trial or at least an evidentiary hearing or immediately release.

CHAPTER 17

FED'S CAMP LIVE

Joiner, 10642-026 report to the unit team office ASAP. As I walked into the office my unit team said, Joiner your point has drop to eleven so that me you are now qualify as a minimum security inmate. I need you to give me three camps that you would like to go to," said Ms. Fields.

"I would like Millington, Tennessee; Terre Haute, Indiana; or Marion, Illinois." While in FCI Oxford I never heard an inmate or guard say anything good about the camp. As a matter of fact, the guards use to tell us that they hated working at the camp, because it was like working with a group of youths and they were always telling on each other. In fact, they said that the camp inmates also told on the guards.

Contrary to the camp gossip floating through the grape vine at Oxford, once I got to the low security institution I heard nothing but good things about the prison camps—"free but not free. They had no fences, somewhat better food, jobs in the community, less security, opportunity to have sex with your girl, and there was very little tension, because nobody wanted to leave the camp and go back behind the fence.

About three months later, I was told that I had been designated to the Federal Prison Camp in Terre Haute, Indiana. The night before I was shipped out, I stayed up all night thanking and praising God for watching over me and not allowing anything to happen to me. Just knowing that I was headed to the camp gave me a sense of peace, hope and I could see a light of freedom. I had begun to feel like I was a changed person with hope and opportunities ahead of me.

My son Jr and my daughter Lynnikia visiting me on Christmas Day in 2002.

Giving closing remark to the audience about a stage play that I wrote and
presented to my fellow inmates & staff title "I DON'T FIT IN ANYMORE"

MOM & POPS doing time with me mentally and spiritually.
My backbones, they did every day with me.

On the morning of September 10, 2003 I was on the BOP bus headed to Terre Haute Prison Camp without any shackles on me. It had been seven years for me behind the fence. During the trip, all I could do was stare out of the window at a changed world with all kinds of new vehicles rolling along, and I noticed the stores and buildings. I felt lost in society just by seeing the changes, but I also saw the sight of freedom that seemed like a long time coming. After dozing off for a few minutes, I woke up and saw a sign that read: Oxford, Wisconsin ahead. Moments later we were at FCI Oxford, the place where I had started my time. The guard called everyone's name, except for me and three other guys. He told us to stay on the bus.Once the guards returned to the bus, they told us that we were going over to the camp. As we arrived at the Camp, it reminded me of the John Hayes Homes Community Center where I use to work.

The camp only had about two hundred and fifty inmates. Most of them were blue collar guys', police officers, and politicians.

There was a few dudes there that I knew from FCI Oxford, like Bubble Eyes.

He looked out for me on food and the telephone. He had his own personal cellphone.While Bubble-Eyes was showing me around there was guys running in and out of the building. Some of them had McDonald's while others had Popeye's Chicken. I only knew one guard, and he was a kitchen police who I had known previously from my stay at the FCI medium joint.

"Joiner, I need a good head cook, so make sure that you ask to be in the kitchen on the A.M. cook shift."

"Okay, Slick Rick, as soon as I get to Terre Haute, I will do just that,"

I replied with a smile on my face. Then Rick walked over to me.

"So you're not staying here? Where are you headed," asked Slick Rick?

"I'm going to the camp in Terre Haute, Indiana. I wasn't joking when I said that I'd do it as soon as I get there."

"I wish you were staying here, but on the other hand, it's nice to see you and take care of yourself."

Around 5:30 a.m., a guard came by my bed.

"Joiner, I need you to get up and get ready. The bus will be here in about twenty minutes.

"Yes Sir," I replied. After getting myself together, I went and tapped on Bubble-Eye's bed to let him know that I was leaving.

As the bus pulled up, I was so use to being shackled down, the guard had to tell me to go on and get on the bus, because I was standing there actually waiting for someone to put shackles on me. It had totally slipped my mind that I had arrived at Oxford Camp with no shackles. There were about thirty five guys on the bus when I made my way aboard. About three of them were secured in a black box to go along with their shackles. A black box is a special set of handcuffs consisting of a very thick and flat black black bar in the middle so that your hands are immobilized. This uncomfortable device is placed on dangerous and high risk inmates who mostly have life sentences. During the trip to MCC Chicago, the guard bumped the radio all the way to our destination. As we pulled into the parking lot, a beautiful young, slim f~ guard came out of the building and the prisoners on the bus went wild. They were banging on the window, whistling and praising her with all kinds of foul language like . . . "look at that bad 'B', whore, MF, and DS." One guard on the bus yelled for the men to calm down.

It' s just a female, and she hates inmates," he stated. A few minutes after the guard had rained on the guys parade, the Lieutenant came onto the bus and barked a few instructions.

"Everyone with shackles on are staying here. So, when I call your name, come up here and give me your name and register number." All thirty five guys that was on the bus when I got on it in Oxford got off the bus at MCC Chicago.

Guess what, thirty five guys came out of the building and got on the bus with me. They all had on shackles except for two of them who were going to the camp with me.

As we made our way onto 1-94 Freeway, all of a sudden it got very quiet on the bus, so I looked at everybody. They were all staring out of the window.

I could tell that it had been a while since most of the guys, as well as myself had seen the outside world. All of us cherished every second of the brief sight of momentary freedom. We stared out of the window at Lake Michigan, looking at all of the tall buildings and the late model vehicles.

We eyeballed the beautiful women that were riding along in the vehicles. Most of us couldn't even identify the names and models of the cars due to being caged up so long.

When we arrived in Terre Haute, Indiana, I saw a sign that read" Terre Haute Federal Penitentiary. As we got inside of the horrific looking penitentiary wall, a guard walked ahead of the bus, directing the driver to the inmates receiving area. I'm almost free, I told myself. Once we were inside of the institution, the guard took me and the other two guys that were going to the camp in the back and finger printed us. Then we were given a new set of bus pants and at-shirt. After we got dressed, we were seen by a PA and a case manager, who assigned us to a unit at the camp. I was assigned to A-Unit. They gave me a bed roll and transported me to the camp. I knew some of the homies, plus some familiar faces were there from Waseca.

As I left the Guard's Station to go to my unit, I ran into my guy, Black Peter. We had done time together in Oxford as well as Waseca He walked me to my bunk area. I threw my bed roll on my bunk and Peter gave me a tour of the camp. After leaving the gym, we went to the kitchen, which happened to be very small. Just as I walked through the kitchen door I heard a familiar voice . . .

"My nephew, shouted my uncle Tommy-T! "What's up boy? How come you didn't call your aunt Peggy and let her know that you was headed here?"

Left: Terre Haute Federal Prison

In 2003, he was transferred to the Federal Prison camp in Terre Haute, Indiana where he became the group leader of an outreach program called "CHOICES." The inmates would go to every elementary, middle and high school as well as the Juvenile Center and Boys and Girls Club that was within a 100 mile radius of the institution.

"Because I wanted to surprise you like I did," I said.

"We can use you here in the kitchen," he told me.

"You know working in food service is my thing," I replied.

"I get off work at about 5:30 p.m. I'll hook you up when I get off . . . better yet, here's the combination to my locker." Once Uncle Tommy-T got off work, he gave me everything that I needed, such as soap, toothpaste, toothbrush, deodorant, shampoo, shower shoes, shorts and a radio. After TommyT took his shower and got himself situated, we toured the camp. He showed me all of the homies and introduced me to some of his friends. Most of the guys at the camp were from the state of Indiana.

It shocked me at the fact that there was no razor wire, no fences, and no gun towers. The place had inside and outside basketball courts. It had a tennis court, baseball diamond, and there were weights in the basement and outside. There was also a large garden on the east side of the yard for the inmates. They grew watermelon, cantaloupes, bell peppers, yellow peppers and corn. There was no air condition at the camp, and the televisions were down in the gym area instead of in the units. We were allowed to watch TV and institutional movies in the visitation room when there was no visitation.

Visiting days were Friday, Saturday, Sunday, and Monday. Most of the guards who worked visitation would allow you to take your lady friend in the men's restroom for ten minutes for a fifty dollar tip. Now, I must keep it real with you, despite all of the great benefits at the Fed camps, things that you will never see at the low, medium, and USP level, you are still doing time! Being at the camp tested my self control and challenged me on a day to day basis, mentally. I could feel and taste freedom so close, but yet so far, because I still had ten years left to do on my sentence.

I was assigned to an eight man cell. All of the guys introduced themselves to me and made me feel comfortable and very welcome. They were all cool and had great sense of humor. I made a mistake in telling them that I could cook. Boy did they take full advantage of that. I had to tell them that I couldn't cook their personal meals for them every day, but I would do it two days per week and on the weekends. We would make fried rice, wraps, pizza bowls fried noodles, and nachos. Since I was only a couple of hours away from home, my family came to visit me almost every weekend.

After being made aware of the guards who would allow me to take my girls into the men's restroom, I couldn't wait until one of my baby mom's came to visit me. My girl, Evelyn had promised to come and visit me since she only lived about three hours away, and we might be able to be alone for about ten minutes.

The food in the camp chow hall was good. I rated it top of the line prison food. They served steak, chicken parts in which I hadn't had a chicken breast in nearly ten years. They also served real hamburger patties, meatloaf, cornish hens, lasagna, turkey breast, and corn beef. I couldn't wait to join the cook shift and show off my cooking skills. After going through A&O, I was assigned to the cook shift. I wasted no time show casing my talent. I made cornbread from scratch, and everyone thought it was cake. I probably could sale this recipe to Jiffy, but on the other hand, I will make them at least reevaluate their recipe. Ronnie was the head inmate cook, because he had been working in the kitchen for about five years. He made the worst prison mashed potatoes that I had ever tasted in prison.

About three months after being in the kitchen, I was moved up to A.M. assistant cook amongst the inmates. The same day I was asked to make the baked ziti and garlic bread since Ronnie was off that day. I went into the dry storage room and grabbed eighty pounds of ziti pasta. Then I went into the meat cooler and grabbed a hundred pounds of ground beef. After I got the pasta and meat cooked off, I made a nice thick creamy marinara sauce with crushed tomatoes, onions, fresh garlic, green pepper, and spices as well as a little 'ancient Chinese secret of mine. Ancient Chinese secret is a term used to keep from giving an individual your whole recipe. Once I got the ziti made, I topped the two inch pans off with three types of cheese; American Pepper jack and Pizza mozzarella cheese. The staff and inmates praised the dish. They complimented me on my baked ziti which looked and tasted like a knock-out (fake) lasagna. Since I had earned the name Chef L.J., I had to live up to the hype. Even though staff and inmates was praising me, I would always give the other assistant cooks the credit. Every Wednesday we had French- toast, strawberry or blueberry syrup, bacon, eggs to. order, and oatmeal. I would always make the oatmeal somewhat thick, because the guys liked to add milk and syrup to their oatmeal. My french toast batter was very simple, but delicious:

    180 medium eggs, crack
    10 gallons of milk
    3 pounds of white sugar
    1: quart of· vanilla ··flavor
    1 cup of cinnamon
    1/2 cup of water, warm

Pour eggs into a large mixer bowl, beat at medium speed for 10 minutes or until all yoke are broken down.

Add next two ingredients, reduce speed to low, mix for eight minutes.

Add vanilla flavor, mix for five minutes.

Add cinnamon to warm water, beat 30 seconds with a fork, add slowly to mix while mixing, mix for two minutes.

Guess what? You now know how to make L.J.'s Unique French Toast Batter.

TIP** Use Butternut's Texas Toast White Bread.

My opportunity to be the head cook came nine months later when Ronnie was transferred to another camp near his release address. Since r was now the head cook, r began to show my leadership skills to my co-workers and staff at a far greater level. I began prepping the guys, so that one of them could become my assistant. r showed them how to make oven fried chicken, meat loaf, baked beans, ziti, mac & cheese, pancakes, and french toast batter. r even showed them how to make unique sauce from scratch.

Bridge Rick was my supervisor. He trusted in my leadership and cooking skills. We called him Bridge Rick because he would come to work late just about every morning from a bridge card game. After giving me what r needed for the meals, Rick would go into the office and go to sleep. He would ask us to wake him up if his supervisor or someone came by. r can honestly say that neither I nor my crew never took food from the meal. I stuck to my motto, "feed the guys and I will make sure that Rick or whomever take care of us." I made sure that r kept my word with my crew, because they took care of me. r could be a little messy and quite demanding at times, and they always looked out for me. r hated blue Monday's because we had biscuits and gravy. Some people call it 'shit on the shingle' in the prison world. The bakers would wait until r told them that the gravy would be ready in about fifteen minutes before they put the biscuits in the oven, this way they would be hot butter biscuits that melt in your mouth. We started the gravy by making a roux with flour and butter, then added some beef base and let it cook for fifteen minutes. While letting the roux cook, I went over to the tilt skillet and sauted some chopped onions and green pepper. Then I added the ground beef to the onion and peppers. As the meat turned brown, we drained the excess fat and seasoned it with pepper, garlic powder, and added two cups of worcestershire sauce. We would then let the gravy simmer for about ten minutes and then yell to the bakers to put the biscuits in the oven. The biscuits took twelve minutes to cook. Maybe five minutes later the guard would yell to me . . .

"Joiner, are you ready to roll?"

"Yes sir," I would say. A few minutes later about three hundred hungry guys marched through the chow line. Most of them just wanted the hot butter biscuit with grape jelly and they would grab some oatmeal off of the hot bar.

There were millionaires in my unit who hired me as their personal prison chef. I would take the kitchen food and put my own unique twist on it for my two rich customers. Whenever we had baked chicken, I would make savory or smothered chicken for my customers. I would always prepare them a fresh salad with whatever meal that I made for them. I would use fresh lettuce, tomatoes, eggs, cucumbers, cheese, turkey, chicken, or tuna for the meat.

I would always throw in a small cup of my Unique Ranch and Thousand Island dressings that I made from scratch. Once a month my customers would have me to fill out a grocery list for them and they would give it to their family members at visitation. That night, they would meet the runner at the cemetary with the black trash bag filled with the items that I ordered. They would pay me five hundred bucks each month. I would send the money to my children for school clothes, shoes, and their birthdays. I would also use the money to pay for the college courses that I was taking.

Even though cooking in prison was the focal pint of my prison life, I began to think how I could help my children and other youths not to make the same mistakes that I had made. Therefore, I joined the Inmates Teenage 'Choices' Program that was sponsored by the Camp Administrator. There were eight of us inmates that were in the Choices Program. We were escorted to local middle and high schools, juvenile center, youth maternity homes, and community centers to talk to at risk kids about the choices that we had made and about the decisions they were making. Our message was that we didn't want them to end up in jail or prison like us. We shared our stories of how we wound up in prison by the bad choices we had made. We also told them what it was like in prison.

"My name is Lynard Joiner, but my name is now inmate Joiner, 10642-026.

I'm serving a twenty year sentence for conspiracy to distribute cocaine and crack cocaine. I have a daughter who was ten years old when I left the streets, and she will be twenty-eight when I get out. I also left four young sons out there without a father: a six year old, two two year old's, and a three month old. They will all be pretty much grown when I get, so that means they will are growing up without dad . . . ME. My choices didn't only affect me, but it affected my children the most. I won't get the opportunity to seen any of them graduate from high school. My actions also placed them in harms way, because I'm not able to be there and teach them to be good decision makers in life. I'll make it really clear that myself, nor my fellow inmates are here because we're getting paid. We are simply here because we love and care about each of you. Y'all are our future judges, lawyers, doctors, police officers, politicians, chefs, school teachers, NBA stars, NFL stars, movies stars, or whatever you dream or desire to be. Most of all, never forget that your education is the key that open the doors of opportunity and path to success. I want you to stand to your feet and point to yourself while repeating after me, "I love myself . . . I am somebody special and I can and I will achieve my goals in life . . . I am a hero and a winner!"

After the section was over I spoke with several of the youth one-on-one. I just Hope that I said something that would help them not to travel down the road of life that I once traveled.

One day I went to an all white high school and spoke to about forty five hundred students. This day, me and three white inmates went out to speak to the youth. Since I was the group leader, I spoke last. As I stood up to speak, all eyes, including the camera was on me. "I know exactly what y' all are thinking. What can this colored man tell us. He has never walked in our shoes. Well, maybe I haven't, but I understand that life is all about choices. There are consequences to our choices, and there are reactions to our own actions. Choices and crimes see no color. There all races in prison, because they didn't make the right choices. I am here today to talk to you about making the right choices, so that you won't make the same mistakes that I made or any of my fellow inmates made. You have the opportunity to be whatever you want to be. I love each one of you and I want you to always believe in yourself and your dreams. Your education is very important to your future success.

Speaking to those youths, especially those that were in juvenile centers and maternity schools gave me peace, a sense of hope, encouragement, and the opportunity to give back to society and help the next generation. The Choices Program also helped me to look deeper within myself and helped me to be a better father, friend and a role model.

A few months later, I was transferred to Millington Camp. I went there in hopes of being reunited with Cheek, but once I got there, he jacked his camp off by getting caught with a cellphone. Upon arriving at Millington Camp, the guard searched me and my property. Then he asked me the routine questions of entering another prison. Once he finished questioning me, he escorted me to my unit, which was B-Unit. Millington Camp was totally different from Terre Haute. Instead of eight man rooms, they had two-man cubicles. The camp was situated on a navy base. There were guys there from the home-front, which was all part of Tennessee, St. Louis, Arkansas, and Mississippi. There were also about forty guys there from all parts of North Carolina, because the Seymore Johnson Prison Camp had closed down, and they were shipped to FPC Millington.

My first job there was working out in the navy community at a catering hall. This job was right up my alley since I had a certificate in catering, and gourmet cooking. I worked with professional chefs, waitresses, and alongside navy cooks. It was a tremendous blessing to me.

In the meantime, I became a very popular inmate in the eyes of the staff and inmates, because of Cheek. I immediately got involved in the Church and shared my spiritual gifts and talents with the Christians brothers. I write plays, skits, and I teach the Word of God. After being at the camp for eight months, I was voted to be the master of ceremony for the Labor Day Family Picnic. I will never forget this experience. The event started at six a.m. and ended at 3:45 p.m. that afternoon. Our families were allowed to come into the camp yard area, which was designated for the picnic. Our family was allowed to bring us whatever food we desired! My mother, pops and several other family members attended the picnic with me. My mother made fried chicken wings, catfish fillet, greens with turkey necks, cornbread, sweet potatoes, three types of cakes including my favorite—sock it to me. We also had red grapes, peaches, and Nehi Peach Soda. The navy base staff donated us tents, tables, games, and prizes for awards to give to the kids for winning special games we did for the event. We also had live music by several different bands. We performed a stage play for the families, it turned out great.

Just leaving Sunday service & counting my blessings and praising God.

After a few changes were made out on the Community Job Detail, I decided to take a job in the education department as a tutor. I loved helping the guys obtain attain their education and seeing life from a whole different perspective. I also taught several self help classes, such as; Positive Mental Attitude (PMA), Breaking Barriers, Parenting, Public Speaking, and Resume Writing. My supervisor believed in me and therefore she gave me the green light. I would have her to bring in volunteers from the outside world to speak on topics such as; HIV / AIDS, Child Support, Credit Reports, and Financial Management.

One of the biggest moments for me at the camp was when I catered the 2006 GED Program Graduation. I really didn't have the best or proper equipment that I needed, but I did the best with what I had. I didn't even have a pastry bag, so I used plastic gloves. I made party chicken wings with BBQ, honey mustard, buffalo, and blue sheese sauce, deviled eggs garnish, with lettuce, cakes, pies, cookies, and a punch with a variety of fresh fruits in it. I also made seasoned potato logs. Good food is always more appetizing when it's properly prepared and served in an appealing presentation. When food is accompanied by garnishes, it changes an ordinary meal into something unique and very special. Therefore, I garnished the tables with palm trees. The branches were made with green peppers. The trunks were made out of carrots, and I made each base with potatoes. I also made garnish out of other fruits and vegetables. After catering the graduation, the praise came in masses from both the inmates and staff. This helped to strengthen my confidence. It felt good to be praised for doing something positive and bringing smiles to people's faces from a positive thing, instead of giving them something to destroy their lives. "Boy, you use to be a damn fool," I said to myself. "But now what are you going to do? Are you going own your own restaurant when you get out?"

Now, on the other hand, I really felt that I was close to being, free.

I had whatever I wanted to eat from the streets mostly everyday. I know you're probably saying shame on me, but it was just one of the benefits of being at the camp. Guys brought food in and we all ate it. There was a vacant house in the neighborhood about fifty yards from the camp. A couple of the inmates went to Wal-Mart and bought some curtains to put in the window. This house became the pizza and package drop off spot for the family and friends that brought the goods. They would drop off bags full of alcohol, cigarettes, tennis shoes, food, and I hate to say it, but even weed sometimes. I didn't smoke, but I just knew what was going on. The people making the drops would call the inmates on their cellphones and let them know that the bag was there. The guys would then jump the three foot fence or pay an inmate runner to go and get the bags. There was also young ladies living in the neighborhood that would come up to the fence and talk with us. During the summer while hanging out in their backyard, some of them would put freak shows on for the inmates.

My guy, Big Mike had gotten released, and he would bring me a big bag to the spot once a week. Most of the time it would be groceries and fast food. I would order about thirty bags of assorted Uncle Ben's 90 Second Rice, Tyson Chicken Pouches, Fruit Cocktails, Velvetta Cheese, Soft Batch Chocolate Chip Cookies, and hygiene products.

My co-worker, Dave, who was a business man, gave me a different perspective to focus on and build upon. "L, J" you got to see life for what it is and follow your vision. A man without a vision will perish. Your future is in your hands, so what are you doing with it?"

A PICTURE OF ME CATERING THE 2006 GED PROGRAM GRADUATION.
KNOWLEDGE IS POWERFUL BEYOND MEASURE.

A few months later, I was transferred to Fort Dix, New Jersey where I completed a four thousand hour industry cooking apprenticeship program with the Department of Labor. After completing the cooking course in April of 2010, I was transferred to the Federal Prison Camp in Atlanta, Georgia. This camp had nothing to offer an inmate who was trying to better himself. In prison, we call this type of camp a death trap, which means the place is set up for an individual to fail. But an inmate must still do the time and don't let the time do you.

It is now 2011 and I have been here at the camp for eleven months and I have lost my sister due to breast cancer, along with brain cancer three days before my birthday. Even though I go home next year, the warden and his staff denied me a furlough and the opportunity to attend my sister's funeral.

A few months later I received a letter from the court stating that I am eligible for immediate release under the retroactive crack guideline Amendment and the Fair Sentencing Act which goes into effect on November 1, 2011. I know coming out of prison is going to be a challenge for me, but I'm up for the challenge, because if God be for me, who can be against me and I have prepared myself to return to the free world and how to stay out of prison.

CHAPTER 18

MY ANGEL

I am a firm believer that sometimes angels comes into our lives and we failed to recognize them at that time. I met a beautiful young lady named Angel when I were seventeen in the John Hay Homes project. She had a great personality with a heart of gold. There was something different about her that made her stand out from the rest of the girls in the neighborhood. I could tell that she came from a well manner family. She looked so innocent.

I took her to be a virgin so I never tried to have sex with her nor did I ever kiss her in a sexual way. To this day I still wonder if she bad-mouthed me to her friend who I knew wasn't a virgin.

"Girl I don't know what's up with LJ. He never want to kiss or try to have sex with me. All he want to do is walk and hold my hand, said Angel.

"The country boy might be scare of the city pussy girl.
Said Jane.

You can rest assure that I wasn't scare. If anything I let her innocent church girl personal fooled me. Nevertheless I decided to leave Angel and chased girls that I knew wasn't a virgin.

About four or five years later I ran into Angel again. One day while working at the United Way, my supervisor called me into the main office. As I walked into her office I seen a beautiful young lady sitting at her desk typing her heart out. All of a suddenly my supervisor said, "Hey LJ, I'm over here."

After seeing what my supervisor wanted I went over to the young lady desk. As I got closer she looked like Angel.

"What's up? I know you are not who I think you are."

"All depend who you think I am mr LJ" she said.

"I think you are Angel, My use to be girlfriend in the John Hayes Homes."

"So you done forgot how I look. I knew you didn't like me for real." She said.

Yes I did but I were immature back then girl. I am a man now baby.

She wasn't trying to hear nothing that I had to say. It were written all over her face and in her voice that she were salty with me about the way that I played her.

"Are you still trippin on what happen between us in the past? I'm trying to get with you now girl."

"LJ, I'm not mad with you but I were disappointed on the way that you played me."

Check this out, I must get back to work. What time is your lunch break? "Why? It's at noon." She said I will be waiting on you at the front door.

About twenty minutes later she came out of the building looking real sexy So where are you trying to have lunch at?

"I got a taste for some Pizza hut.' She said As we walked over to Pizza Hut and got in line to order she said'

"Could we have to separate order please?

"Excuse me, it all going to be on the same ticket. I'm paying for it.'

After we order the food we went found us a table in the back of the restaurant so we could talk in private. The first thing that came out of her mouth were, "I am involved with someone and I don't believe in cheating on my man or playing with his feelings.

I can respect that baby-girl.

"So are you still with that one light skinned girl and don't act like you don't know who I am talking about? ".

I am a free man and my own man too.

After talking to Angel for about fifteen minutes longer and getting nowhere we headed back to the job site. I asked her for her seven digit but she wouldn't give it to me nor her address. One day I decided to follow her home from a distance. While riding around one night I went by Angel house. I pulled up into the driveway and blew my horn. She came to the door and said, "Who is it?"

I didn't say a word, I just stared at her standing in her doorway. A few minute later I pulled off. This were the last time that I saw Angel before I went to prison.

The most favorite time of the day in prison for most guys beside chow-time is mail—call or love-call. One day while standing at mail-call, I got a piece of mail with the name Wonderful Angel on it. As I received it I said who in the world is this. I don't know nobody by this name that live in springfield. I will read it when I get back from school or before I go to bed.

In prison it me more than anything to you to get a letter, pictures and a few dollar on your book. Sometime in prison it can seem like you are dead and nobody care.

There's a saying that is popular in prison that say. "out of sight, out of mind."

Most of the guys and women in prison rather get a letter from their girl or lovesone than a few dollars on their book knowing that they are not going to starve in prison. You are going to get three square meals a day. This doesn't mean that you will like them but they are there for you.

As I got back from school and open and read the letter that I had got early, the letter was from my angel Angel. I never knew her name were Angel. In the letter she told me that she got my info from my niece Trisha who work with her and she also looked me up on the internet.

I quickly wrote her back to say thanks and asked her to be my pen-pal. She replied ASAP and told me that she was involved with somebody but she is willing to be my pen-pal. As time passed our relationship begin to change from pen pal to friends with benefits. She begin to write me more and be more supported to me in all aspect. Therefore I felt that I need to be up-front and truthful with her and hope that she would do the same with me. One of the biggest things that guys in prison does when he met a woman or reunited with an ex is lie about his release date. As for myself I told Angel my true release day.

In Angel four letter to me she asked me "Why didn't you try to find me before you went to prison?

"I became a drug dealer and my love and respect for you wouldn't allow me to get involve with you knowing my criminal lifestyle plus I didn't want to ruin your life like I almost done mine.

"I want you to know that I appreciate you and respect you even more now." she said.

I am one that believe that God bring people back into your life for a reason, season, or a lifetime. When that special someone come back into your life for a Reason, they are back to take care of some unfinished business, meet a special need that you have, help you through a hard time and provide you with guidance whether it be mentally, physically or spiritually. She may seem like an angel sent from above better yet she is. All of a suddenly they leave without a reason which mean they had completed their reason.

When that special someone come back into your life for a Season, they are back because your time has come to give, show a sign of mature and learn from them and appreciate them more than you did the first time. They provide you with an experience of peace like never before and cause you to laugh when there's no clown around. They also give you a sense of unspoken joy.

All of a suddenly that special someone disappear without a reason but on the other hand, their season work has come to an end in your life.

When a special someone come back into your life for a Lifetime, nine out of ten times they are back to grow old and gray with you. They will teach you a lifetime of things that the two of you must build upon in order for the relationship to last a lifetime. A relationship growth is a day to day process because you can rest assure that there are going to be some rainy days in your relationship meaning good and bad days. I once heard an old farmer tell his son who wife had put him out that a relationship is like planting crops, if it never rain, nothing will ever grow.

I hope it didn't go over your head. I want you to know that special someone can come back into your life for a Reason which turns into a Season and becomes Lifetime.

Every night before I go to sleep, I give God thanks for bringing Angel back into my life. All the guys here in prison tell me that I must be a lucky guy to have a woman like Angel by my side in this circumstance. My response to them is, "I'm not lucky. I'm blessed to have her by my side."

One thing about being in prison especially with a long sentence, people will, turns their back on you and this include your family, lovesone, so-called best friend, girlfriend, and baby-mom.

There are a lot of guys in here that don't have anybody by their side and I mean nobody for whatever reason. Therefore I counts my blessings that I have a family that care and an angel by my side.

When I sit and think about how and why we are reunited, it all started with a pup love nearly thirty years ago. At that time we really didn't know how to express ourselves. I am now older, wiser, matured and know what type of woman that I am looking for and need in my life.

Angel seem to be that woman who has came back into my life for a season, reason and I pray for a Lifetime but only time will tell. I hope that you will recognize your angel when she come along.

CHAPTER 19

THE FORK IN THE ROAD AHEAD

I can't believe that I am about to get out of prison after serving nearly seventeen years. I am happy and I am very confident, not cocky that I have prepared myself for the challenge of returning to the free world and how to stay out there. I would like to thank God for watching over me all throughout my imprisonment and taking care of my mother, pops, children, and my family as a whole while I was on my journey through the valley to the kitchen.

It's time for me to put up or shut up, because I am about to face the toughest challenge of my life once I hit the free world as we call it here in prison. I must also walk the sermon that I've preached here in prison to myself and other guys. There's a saying that says, "actions speak louder than words, because the mouth is made to say anything. I'm not coming out of prison thinking that it's going to be a cake-walk for me, because I know a lot has changed and I must start all over because I have no money, clothes, transportation nor a house to go to. There's nothing like your own, no matter how much someone give you or make you welcome.

. I can honestly say that one thing that I didn't do were took my imprisonment to be a place where I could tighten up my hustling game. I used it as a place where I could learn from my mistakes, repent, and become a mature man, a better son, father, as well as a better individual in society and life. I now know that life is not all about me. It's much bigger than me. God has blessed me in my present circumstance, so I can come out of prison and bless others. I now know that my life has value, purpose, and meaning. It doesn't include selling drugs, killing, stealing, hurting people, or mistreating women, nor blaming society for my past actions. I have now accepted my responsibility for the crime that I committed and I am moving on with my life. I understand that the deck may be stacked against me and I know it's going to be tough and I know it's going to be super tough, but God is on my side. There's nothing to hard for Him! I know that the road back to society and to success is not going to be easy. There are going to be bridges called relationships that I am going to have to rebuild, re lights called haters, pot holes called so-called friends, flashing lights called loved ones, curves called fear, one-way streets called confusion, and forks in the road called choices. Therefore I must have faith, patience, determination, perseverance, self discipline, and believe in myself.

I can't go back into the free world and do the same things that I was doing that got me in this predicament. You can't do the same thing that got you into prison and expect a different result, it's not going to happen, so that is insanity to think that way. The old self or image man that died during my incarceration, I must not breathe life back into him. I must kill him daily. You may not agree with me, but I am of this persuasion, I don't have to prove to anybody that I am a changed person except myself, because if I prove it to myself, everyone else is going to be able to see the change in me. On the other hand, people are going to remember me as who I was before I came to prison and say all types of negative things about me, which I have no problem with, because I am not who or what they say I am. I am who I believe that I am. One thing that I know without a doubt, I am not the lost, uneducated, confused, and blind person that I was when I first came in here. r recall an old head telling me, "L.J., you have to get out of prison before you are released from prison, or you will be right back," he said to me. Even though r really didn't understand what the old guy was really telling me at that time, his words took root in my mind. As I pondered on the older gentleman's words from time to time. I guess he was telling me that just to say that leaving prison doesn't necessarily mean that my mind is free from prison, and that could cause me to get back into trouble. I know that I must find new friends or should I say, new associates. I certainly can't afford to hang out with my old so-called friends, especially those who are still doing the same old thing that we did when I left the streets. I must have the courage to tell them that I don't fit in anymore. I understand that they may call me scary, square, soft, or church boy. That's okay. They can call me whatever they like and place whatever tag they want to put on me, but I will be free and full of the joy of the Lord.

I don't have another bid in me, plus I have already robbed my children of a father in the most critical stages of their lives. Time is a precious commodity, because once it's gone, you can never get it back. Therefore, I am not able to give any time back to my children and my family as a whole, but I pray that they will find it in their heart to forgive me and allow me to be a blessing to them by sharing my talents, skills, and what God has done in my life through words, but mostly through my actions. I am going to live a productive life, be a positive influence in my community, and make a positive contribution to society by the grace of God. Yes, it's going to be a battle, but the battle won't be mine, but the Lord's. I will continue to stay on the battle field. I refuse to give up and sale myself short of an opportunity to be the man that God created me to be in the beginning. Even though weapons are going to be formed against me, they will not prosper. God's angels are going to always encamp around me and protect me from all harm and danger. I know that God did not bring me this far, through so many years of imprisonment for no reason. He has a plan and a purpose for my future life out in the free world.

God took my mess and turned it into a blessing and a message.

Wherefore, just as a butterfly struggles to free itself from its cocoon, so have I struggled to free myself from the world and environment that I existed in for so long. I am ready to travel down the road of life again with the fork in it but this time will be different because I now have a sense of direction, purpose, and meaning to my life which me that I know my true self worth.

CHAPTER 20

BACK TO SOCIETY

Joiner!10642-026, bring all of your property to R & D immediately. your sentence has been reduced and you are entitle to be release immediately. As I were walking to R&D with a couple of my guys helping me with my property and hundreds of others inmates looking at me with the "I wish it were me look on their face" all I could say, "were stay strong and focus yall time is coming soon."

Once I got to R & D the butterflies of fear of the unknown begin to fill my stomach. I gave my guys a hug and some dap. As I got inside the counselor told me to come into her office. She then verified my release address and my name. I were then giving the money that I had on my book, a greyhound bus ticket and $25.00 to purchase three meals on my way home. I was then taken to the bus station and drop off by the inmate cab driver.

While sitting at the bus station waiting on my bus to Nashville Tennessee, it felt like all eyes were on me. I tried to stay cool and calm or should I say that I tried to fit in with society but I stuck out like a sore thumb with my gray prison Russell sweat suit on. While waiting on the bus a couple of people came over and talked to me. I were very surprised that neither of them asked me where I were coming from but they all asked where I was going. I told them that I were headed to Springfield, Illinois. Most of them was going to Saint Louis. As the bus came up and I went to grab my bags, a nice looking young lady came up and asked me did I need any help with my baggies. I told her that I were ok.

Once we got on the bus she asked "What is your name and can I sit with you?"

"Sure you can and my name is LJ," I said.

So what is your name young lady? I asked "M y name is Terri and I am older than you think I am." She said.

"You can't be no more than twenty eight," I said.

She then reached into her purse and pulled out her driving license and gave it to me. She looked even younger on her ID. Nevertheless she were forty four according to her ID. After having a general conversation for about an hour Terri fell asleep on my shoulder. I must admit that all kind of sexually thoughts ran through my mind especially with me having been lock-up for nearly seventeen years. My joint were harder than a rock but I stay under control with Angel on my mind. I want Angel to be my first coming out of prison.

Once we got close to Nashville I woke Terri up. She quickly went to opologing and explaining herself to me. "LJ, I am so sorry. I normal don't go asleep around stranger especially on a strange man shoulder"

It's all good but remember there is always a first time for everything. and I believe that you can meet a perfect stranger.

Terri looked at me and said, "Do you really believe that?

"Yes I do believe it with all of my heart", I said After leaving Nashville we headed to Evavston, Indiana in which we had a three hours lay-over. The station were closed as we arrived there at about 4;00 am. We all just went and sat on the side of the building. It was cold as hell out there. You could hear us shilling out there. Terri and I tried to keep each other warm.There were nobody out and not a gas station or restaurant in sight.

The next bus that showed up were headed to St Louis which meant I were getting closer to my designation. Once again Terri and I sat together which was our last sat together because St Louis were her designation. As we got off the bus we went and had breakfast at McDonald's that were across the street from the bus station. While having breakfast Terri gave me her phone number and address and told me to get at her.

As we left St Louis and headed to Springfield I stared out of the window with fear of the unknown and changes that has taken place while I were on my journey begin to creep in. Nevertheless I kept telling myself, You have done the hard part and prepared yourself for the challenge. So don't give up on your mission and dreams and they want give up on you. A man once told me that fear is nothing but false expectation that appear to be real.

You may not believe it but I didn't even recognized Springfield at first until I seen the Stevenson Drive sign. WOW! Look at Springfield., I said to myself. I was so amazed at all of the changes and growth of the city since I had left. As the greyhound bus pulled up into the station, I grabbed my bags and made my way off the bus. I immediately went to the phone and called my son Zo to come get me. About twenty minute later a young man with threds and a cute young later came into the station looking around. I said to myself those must be my children. So I got up and walked over to them. The young lady said, 'Lyn!

What up Precious? The young man wasn't my son. He were my nephew Malcoln. They told me that Zo were at home. We then got into the car and went over to Zo house.

As we got to the house and went knock on the door a young man with threds came to the door. We looked at each other for about twenty second and gave one another a big hug. He then introduced me to his girlfriend. I couldn't believe that my son Zo had grown up and had his own family.

After spending time with Zo, I went to visit my son Junior. I immediately recognized Junior as I walked into the house. We gave each other a hug and he grab his coat and went with me over to my sister house. While at my sister house Junior bought me up to speed on what going on in the city as well as the family. What Junior didn't know where that several family member and friends has told me about his activities which wasn't good. I waited for him to tell me but I guess his pride and not knowing how I would take it or react wouldn't let him tell me. Nevertheless he hung out with me mostly every day for the first couple of months that I were out.

About 9:oop hat night Angel came over to my sister and got me. As she knocked on the door and came in, I said "Hello Angel, how are you doing?"

"I'm good". She said.

I could tell that she was shame and not comfortable being in the house. So I told her that I would be ready in a few minute. Once I got dressed, I told junior that I will catch up with him later. I then told vetta let go. As we got outside she asked me for a hug. I gave her a big hug and a kiss on the cheek. We then walked on over to her new truck which were a Mercedes-Benz.

"WOW!, Life must be treating you good baby-girl."

"I guess you can say that but on the other hand I have work for everything that I got." She said.

I take my hat off to you sweetheart and I am a firm believe that when you work for something you appreciate it and value it more.

As we pulled up into her driveway and went inside of her house I was very impressed with how nice it looked. She immediately went into her bedroom and put on something comfortable. Once she came back out we sat on the couch and watched tv and just tried to feel each other out since we haven't seen each other in nearly twenty-five years. After talking for about three hours she told me that she were going to bed because she had to be at work at 6;00am. I told her to give me a pillow and some cover so I could chill on the couch. I really wanted to sleep with her but at the same time I didn't want to give her the wrong impressing even though she probably wanted some sex like me. I couldn't wait to go the bed the next night so I could rock her world if you know what I mean. That night took me back to my first time having sex. Since it had been so long since I had some sex it didn't take me long to get my rock off. A few days later I moved in with Angel and she immediately gave me a house key and a small bankroll to put in my pocket. If you have a good woman guys I encourage you to keep her and treat her like a queen because if you don't someone else will.

After being out for a month and a half I being to focus on my plans, mission and goals that I made in prison. I begin to go into the school, juvenile center and communities centers sharing my lie story and speaking to youth about life choices. My life story made the front page of the Springfield newspaper and I appeared on several local radio talk shows as well as one in Dallas Texas and Memphis Tennessee. As a man of my words and my love for the prison brotherhood, I sent newspaper articles of my story to all of the federal prison where I served time at not to boast but to encourage and give the guys some hope. I also send positive message back into the system telling the guys to prepare themselves for their return back to society educational, mentally, physically and spiritually because the individual who fail to plan, plan to fail In January 2012, I formed a self supported Not-for-Profit organization called H-YARD (Helping Youth at Risk Develop) The program mission is to educate at risk youth on life choices and the consequences of their choices and help them develop into positive individuals in life. I am currently a head-cook at a hotel and seeking to have my own restaurant open soon with help from the small business center. Just in case you are wondering, yes I am still on supervised release doing all these positive things. Therefore I am a firm believer that the only someone that can put a limit on you is YOU. I refused to let anybody hold me back especially myself. I would also like to free your mind about it hard to get a job being an ex-con. That is somewhat true but on the other hand if nobody else will hire you, hire yourself. You can start your own motivational speaking business in which you can charge organization for sharing your life story or experience. If you have a trade you can open your own business in that field of work. I can say it from experience there are opportunities out here in the free world even though some have more tha Others but nevertheless you must be ready and willing to take advantage of the opportunity that come your way. There's an old saying that say "If you stay ready, you don't have to get ready if you know what I mean."

If you don't remember nothing else that I said in this chapter please remember this, if you are in prison and is about to be release please don't come out here thinking that you must prove yourself to anybody except yourself because you will lose focus on what self need to do. If you prove it to self everyone else will see the reflection and results. Your past is only your past when you keep it as your past and not your future or an excuse,.

AFTERWORD

My beautiful sister Annie

After battling breast and brain cancer for a while, my sister Annie died on May 15, 2011 and I were released from prison on November 1'2011.

I remember going to check my e-mail, and as I opened it, it read, "L.J., I'm sorry, it's Annie, she is dead. As I sat at the computer, tears began to roll down my face. This is the worst mail or news that you can get while in prison, that a loved one is dead.

My sister Annie's death crushed me even though I told the family that I was okay and I will be alright. Annie was a motherly type of sister to me.

She was very humble, calm, cool, and had a great sense of humor. But on the other hand, it wasn't good to bring out the other side of her.

The next day after Annie's death, I went to my case manager's office and requested a furlough to attend Annie's funeral. My case manager had me to do all of the requirements that was needed in order for me to attend her funeral.

A day before I was scheduled to leave, I was told that the warden of the prison camp denied me because I was a danger to the community, since I had a leadership role in my case. I told my unit team, "You guys got to be joking.

How can I be a danger to the community? I'm at a camp. I can leave whenever I want to. There is nothing to keep here, other than the love for my family, because if it wasn't for them, I would leave. The only thing that y'all can do is lock me up once when I get back and transfer me."

Most of the staff members that work in the federal prison system have no heart, and they lack concern for you or your family. They try to look down on you, but they fail to realize that the only difference between themselves and an inmate is a choice, because no one is exempt from making a bad choice.

Since I wasn't allowed to attend Annie's funeral, I wrote a piece called "Life Never Tell Us The When's or Why's, But God Knows Best."

Sister, Life never tells us the when's or why's, but God knows best, and He has called you home before I got there. So to you, sister/friend, I say thanks for the love you've always shown us, and thanks for your teaching, wisdom, understanding, and most of all, your spirit of unity that you always provided to the family. I wish that I would have had a chance to tell you face to face how much I love you and appreciate you as a sister and a friend, but God knows best.Thanks for never closing the door of your house to me and the family as a whole, especially on holidays. Sister, I know that you're gone, but you will never be forgotten.

I now take the comfort in the words spoken by Dr. Martin Luther King Jr. at the funeral of the four little girls killed in a church bombing in Birmingham, Alabama. He said that . . . "Death is the irreducible common denominator, it does not see color, it does not see age, it does not see religion, it does not see your net worth, it does not see your social status, the only thing it sees is the order it was given by God to bring you to Him at this appointed time." Life never tells us the when's or why's, but God knows best sister Annie.

Sister, your work here on earth is done and you have served your purpose on earth. Therefore sister, I know you were just hanging on as a loan to us from God. God has now taken you back, so who are we to question God? God knows best, sister.

Sister, life was God's way of loaning you to us and death is His way of getting you back. Sister, you will be greatly missed, but I promise you that we will be fine, because your impact on our lives and your contributions to the family is far greater than your life span here on earth could ever show.

The seeds that you planted in our lives and other lives are being seen here in the church today.

Personally sister, you taught me a lot of things and inspired me day after day with your endless kindness. I will see you in glory. So sister, in closing, I will leave you with these words, "Death is not a period, it's a comma. I love you sister, now rest in peace. Your brother, Lyn AKA' L. J."

I love my sister, Annie!

Now that you have read my life story, I pray that you read something that will help you or help you to help someone else so they want make the same mistake or bad choice that I did. Thanks for your support and I just may write LJ'S COCOON 2.

ACKNOWLEDGEMENT

As a young boy, my mother use to always tell me to always remember the people who helped me, inspired me, and supported me. There are countless people who have helped and inspired me in life, before and during my imprisonment, but I can only acknowledge a few of them.

Mother, you have always been by my side since I came into this world.

You've inspired me in a special way day by day. You have always understood me even when I didn't understand myself. Thanks for always keeping our freezer and cabinets full with food and allowing me to steal the food, cook it, and sale it to the children in the neighborhood. Thanks for believing in my dream to become a professional certified cook. Your will power, initiative, and determination lives within me.

Pops, thank you for teaching me how to be a responsible man and how to deal with life's storms. Thanks for providing for me while I was in prison, but most of all, thanks for taking care of my mother and loving her.

To my children, Lynnikia, Lynard Jr., Alonzo and those that only know me to be their dad, I truly apologize for robbing you all of a father in the most critical stages of your lives. I am also sorry for not being there for special events in your childhood. Every day and night I think about how I can give back the lost time to you all, even though I know it's impossible to do. All I can do now is be the best father and friend to all y'all, and the best grandfather in the world to your children.

To all of the positive guys that I met in prison: Thanks for you love, encouragement, inspiration, and constructive criticism.

The Brown's who opened my eyes to the food and business world at the age of thirteen, which kept the fire burning to ignite my dream of becoming a professional cook.

To all of the prison cook foremen, especially at Waseca, Minnesota and Fort Dix, New Jersey, thank you very much.

Last but not least, thanks Wonderful Angel for coming back into my life after nearly thirty years and breathing new life into my lonely heart. Thanks also for your love, care, and support, Thanks for everything.